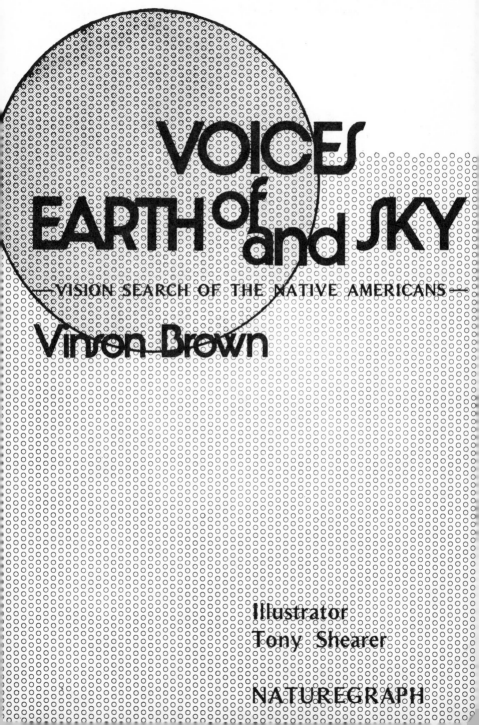

VOICES EARTH of and SKY

—VISION SEARCH OF THE NATIVE AMERICANS—

Vinson Brown

Illustrator
Tony Shearer

NATUREGRAPH

Library of Congress Cataloging in Publication Data ℂℐℙ

Brown, Vinson, 1912–
    Voices of earth and sky.

    Bibliography: p.
    1. Indians of North America—Religion and mythology.
2. Indians—Religion and mythology. 3. Visions.
I. Title.
E98.R3B76 1976   299'.7   76-41761

.

Voices of Earth and Sky was published in a hardcover edition by Stackpole Books and is reprinted by arrangement.

1989 Printing.

Copyright © 1974, 1976 by Vinson Brown

ISBN 0-87961-060-3 Paper Edition

Naturegraph Publishers, Inc., Happy Camp, California 96039

Dedicated to
All people who seek to build harmony, understanding and
spirit among the sons and daughters of men, and to my son,
Kirby Brown, who took Chio Jari's gift of the spirit back to
the Guaymi.

Contents

Acknowledgments   7

Introduction   9

1   **A Song Heard in the Dawn**   13
Learning from Chio Jari, a wild Guaymi of the mountains, and
his Dawn Song

2   **The Spirit Behind Native American Religions**   22
Ecologic and economic basis of religion in America
The shamans or medicine men and the priests of Native American religions

3   **Learning from Mistakes**   31
White people have made innumerable mistakes in dealing with
native peoples of America—their lack of understanding has
been incredible

4   **Learning to Understand and Reach the Spirit**   40
If we dig deep enough to find the eternal power of the spirit
that is within us, we can find the strength to learn from our
mistakes and finally overcome them!

5   **Lords of the Dawn**   48

Real or not real culture heroes—five hypotheses for studying them and searching for the truth

6   **Degandawidah and Hiawatha of the Iroquois**   54

How these two great heroes persuaded the Mohawks, the Oneida, the Cayuga and latter other tribes to join a new religion and form a new League of Nations

7   **The Shining Woman**   61

The story of White Buffalo Calf Maiden of the Sioux—the general patterns of all culture hero accounts begin to emerge

8   **He Who Brought the Sacred Arrows**   68

The story of Sweet Medicine—culture hero of the Cheyennes

9   **The Great Feathered Serpent and the Brotherhood of the Tree**   75

The historical background of the coming of Quetzalcoatl, the Lord of the Dawn, and his great adventure

10   **Out of the Silence They Also Came Singing**   95

Great Central American culture heroes

God-like beings who came to the peoples of western South America

11   **A Sioux Youth Prepares Himself for a Vision**   106

In detail—preparation for a vision search

12   **The Sacred Pipe—Guide to a Vision and to Life**   115

The origins, decorations, fittings and role of the Sacred Pipe in Sioux Indian religion

13   **The Youth Searches for a Vision**   122

An account of a Sioux youth's vision search

14   **The Broken Pipe**   132

The despair of the Indian as all that was beautiful in his past was pulled down and hidden by the curtain of white civilization—the putting away of the Sacred Pipe

15 **Great Dreams Sent by the Above One**   138
The vision of the old Makah
The vision of Black Elk
The vision of the Wishram great-great-grandmother
A great vision of Crazy Horse, holy man and warrior of the Sioux
Chilam Balam, the Great Seer of the last days of the Maya and
his vision of the future of the world

16 **Voices Out of the Earth**   147
A Ute who taught humbleness
The Cheyenne with the face that mirrored the wilderness
A wise and humble Hopi chief
A wise and kind lady
Mad Bear on Indian Youth

17 **Preparing for a Vision Search on Bear Butte**   156
An unusual pipe bag
The Inipi ceremony for healing and purification
Sun Dance of the Oglala Sioux
Prelude to a vision search on Bear Butte

18 **When Fire Rimmed the Sky**   164
Account of the author's vision search on Bear Butte mountain

19 **A Warning from the Thunder Beings**   175
Spiritual strength is needed to help change the world . . . by
love, understanding, purity and the power of example

Bibliography   178

Acknowledgments

THERE ARE SO MANY PEOPLE, organizations or companies that have been helpful in my preparation of this book that I am doubtful I will remember to cover them all in these acknowledgments. I hope the ones I overlook will forgive me and will understand that I am thanking them in my heart.

To Edward Hlauka, Ranger of Bear Butte State Park, South Dakota, thanks is due for the fine photograph of the butte; to my valued Otomi Indian friend and sandpainter, David Villaseñor, for his reading of my manuscript and his excellent suggestions; to Tony Shearer, the Sioux artist, for his beautiful art work and his help on the chapter on Quetzalcoatl; to David Monongye of the Hopi, Mrs. John Stands-in-Timber of the Cheyenne, Edward Box, Sr. of the Southern Utes, Elsie Allen of the Pomo, and Mad Bear Anderson of the Tuscarora, for their suggestions and help with Chapter 16; to Vicky Wright for helping with the typing of the manuscript, and Mrs. Florence Musgrave for her help in securing permissions for the various quotes used in the book; to my wife Barbara, for shielding me from the world when I was concentrating on my writing; to Chio Jari, the wonderful Guaymi Indian of Panama who first started me on the trail that lead to this book; to Frank Fools Crow of the Sioux, chief guide in my vision quest; to David Moore, companion of my vision search, for the story of his three visions; and to all my fine Native American friends who long ago overwhelmingly convinced me of the tremendous value and wisdom to be found in their ancient culture and spiritual heritage.

I wish to acknowledge with thanks also the help I received from all the books listed in the bibliography, but need to give special recognition to the following publishers, authors or their representatives, from whom permission to quote was obtained as applicable: to David Villaseñor for permission to use the quote given at the beginning of Chapter 2, found on page 95 of *Tapestries in Sand*, and to Tony Shearer for his permission to use the quote given at the beginning of Chapter 9, from page 65 of his book, *Lord of the Dawn*, both published by Naturegraph Publishers; to Professor A. Grove Day, compiler of the book *When the Sky Clears* (a selection of Indian poems), for his help in obtaining sources for the following poems: "Darkness Song," at the beginning of Chapter 3, from *Myths and Legends of the Iroquois*, translated by Harriet Converse and edited by Arthur C. Parker, N.Y. State Museum Bulletin 125, December 25, 1908; "Dream Song," at the beginning of Chapter 13, from *The American Indians and Their Music*, by Frances Densmore, New York, 1926; and also "Song of the Sky Loom," at the beginning of Chapter 12, from *Songs of the Tewa*, translated by Herbert J. Spinden, New York, 1933. To the Sierra Club-Ballantine Books, publishers of *Navajo Wildlands*, for their help in obtaining sources for the following: "Dawn Boy's Song," at the beginning of Chapter 4, from *Navajo Myths, Prayers and Songs, with Texts and Translations*, University of California Publications in American Archaeology and Ethnology, Vol. 5, No. 2, Berkeley, 1907; also "Song of the Earth Spirit," at the beginning of Chapter 19, from *Origin Myths of the Navajo Indians*, by Aileen O'Bryan, Smithsonian Institution, Bureau of American Ethnology, Bulletin 163, Washington, 1956. To Dee Seton Barber, Seton Village, N.M., for permission to use the poem reproduced at the beginning of Chapter 16 copied from the top of page 68 of *The World's Rim*, by Hartley Burr Alexander, copyright 1953, by University of Nebraska Press; to Abelard—Schumann, Ltd., and Intext Press, N.Y.C., for permission to use on the last page of Chapter 9, a quotation from page 47 of *The Book of the Jaguar Priest*, by Dr. Maud Makemson, copyright 1951, beginning "On that day—"; to Mrs. Hilda N. Petri, Attorney-at-Law, of Columbia, Missouri, representing the estate of John Neihardt, and the University of Nebraska Press, for the use of quotations used at the beginnings of Chapters 7 and 17, and the Black versity of Nebraska Press; to Abelard—Schumann, Ltd., and Intext Press, N.Y.C., for permission to use on the last page of Chapter 9, a quotation from page 47 of *The Book of the Jaguar Priest*, by Dr. Maud Makemson, copyright 1951, beginning "On that day—"; to Mrs. Hilda N. Petri, Attorney-at-Law, of Columbia, Missouri, representing the estate of John Neihardt, and the University of Nebraska Press, for the use of quotations used at the beginnings of Chapters 7 and 18, and the Black Elk section of Chapter 15, copied from Pages 279-280, and 249-250 of *Black Elk Speaks*, by John Neihardt, University of Nebraska Press, copyright 1932, 1959; to The Hamlyn Publishing Group, Ltd., Middlesex, England for the quotation of Chilam Balam used in the middle of Chapter 9 and taken from p. 93 of *Mexican and Central American Mythology*, by Irene Nicholson, copyright 1967. I am also most grateful for the permission of the Hozansha Publishing Co., Ltd., Tokyo, to quote from the book *Aikido*, as indicated in Chapter 4.

V.B.

Introduction

"Tis strange but true, for truth is always strange—stranger than fiction."

George Noel Gordon, Lord Byron

ONE DAY IN AUGUST, 1972, the cry of "fire!" was heard at our home in the countryside of northern California. When I went outside, I saw great clouds of dark smoke boiling up over the hilltops to the west. I put on a backpack loaded with four gallons of water and a squirting hose and started up the hill to try to help our neighbors there before the fire reached them. As I moved close by the woods above our home, I saw the flames crest the high ridge above like dancing, crimson devils, and there was a great roaring.

And yet all about me at the same time there seemed to be a strange and frightening silence. Then I felt as I had never felt before the trees beside me—felt them crouching, pulling in their powers, almost trembling as a wild animal crouches and prepares for a fight to the death when some great and fierce enemy is about to leap upon it. The feeling was so strong that the hair rose on the back of my neck and I turned half expecting to see the trees take animal form and crouch as my senses suggested. And then the wind was whining in their leaves and I knew *they knew* that death was coming!

One time it would have been foolish to tell anyone about such an experience for the answer would have been only derisive laughter, but recent experiments in New York and Maryland with the highly sensitive instrument known as the lie detector or polygraph have proved to scientists that plants actually do have such feelings and manifest them. Some people sense these feelings, while others don't, but now we have real proof of their existence.

I tell this story at the beginning of the book because some of the experiences, sensations and ideas expressed in the pages that follow are based on feelings that may not yet be explainable in scientific terms or with proofs, but just as the feelings of trees were for years a truth not explainable, so may we be nearing proofs on other hidden truths involving life relationships.

When dealing with the subject of visions and the vision search among the Native Americans, I believe it's possible to write about the subject on the basis of known facts, yet quite probably not achieve any real depth of understanding about the subject. How this can happen is recounted in an episode of anthropological research (Chapter Three). But it is obvious the subject of visions is an extremely subjective matter. I feel I must therefore deal with it on the basis of my gut experience, on what I feel deeply. In doing so I do not expect the reader to take what I say as dogma, but instead regard it as an exploratory path that I sincerely hope will lead to deeper insight. After all, the Indians themselves once talked about how trees and other plants had feelings and a way of communicating, as several histories of early white-Indian contacts imply; but they soon found out the white strangers were totally unsympathetic to such ideas, laughing at them as childish and savage nonsense.

Yes indeed "truth is always strange—stranger than fiction!"

One thing I shall try to do in this book is to show the reader patterns, repeated patterns found in my experience and those of others, that will give evidence of truths or laws of human experience and the existence of feelings behind such patterns. Patterns are used in scientific research to establish natural laws. Thus such scientists as Darwin and Huxley and

Wallace found the same patterns of the use of camouflage by wild creatures repeated in many parts of the world, and found that even on isolated islands in the oceans, the patterns of flightless birds and of animals which actually there needed no camouflage for protection against predators were nevertheless repeated again and again. From such repeated patterns they could prove beyond very little doubt the existence of natural laws of life causing such phenomena to prevail.

Many people will become aware of the presence of a sixth sense, either in themselves or others, or both, if they watch themselves and others very closely. The most obvious way is to notice how often people will turn and look at you when you are observing them closely even though you have not made the slightest noise and there would have been no way for them to know you were in that place at the time. You also, as I have many times, may be walking down the street and suddenly be aware that you are being watched from behind. If you turn quickly, sure enough, there will usually be a person somewhere behind staring at you. Similar experiences are widespread. For example, about four o'clock one night I woke up with the very strong impression that my wife was urgently calling me, but I heard no sound. I went into our office where she had stayed up late to work and found her looking for something. She was surprised to see me, but said she had been calling me in her mind because she thought I might help her find the missing object. I quickly found it for her and went back to bed amazed at the thought transference between us. Yet this is only one of many examples in our family.

Actually our sensitivity to the thoughts and feelings of other people, creatures and even plants can be increased by practice and by working to be more alert and sensitive. The ancient inhabitants of America, who lived close to nature all their lives, and who believed deeply in the sentient nature of all living things, were usually more aware of feelings and thoughts in other beings than we are. Yet each of us, I feel sure, having the same types of brain and nerve cells, are capable of developing these psychic and spiritual powers. It is indeed strange that we have what we call a Holy Bible that tells of many such psychic and spiritual experiences and visions, and yet our own civilization has become so practical and materialistic that most such phenomena are ignored or scorned. We indeed need to ask ourselves if spiritual growth is not what the world today needs far more than additional fancy gadgets!

When I was a young man before and up through the Eisenhower Administration in the United States in the 1950's, such a question would largely have been ignored, for most people saw stretching before us a long time of growth in spectacular scientific discoveries, new gadgets, new cars, more freeways, space flights, and on and on. But today both older and younger generations are becoming increasingly aware that our civilization and its doctrine of striving for material worth and comfort are failing to meet or answer the really deep and lasting needs of mankind and that we are hurtling forward with our increasing pollution, population explosions, crime, wars, riots and other signs of disharmony to a meeting place with destiny that could be extremely uncomfortable if not completely disastrous for us all.

The Native Americans are the people of Earth and Sky. For untold generations they have been dwelling on these two great continents of the western hemisphere largely in harmony with their environment and with far less conflict and disharmony between nations than has been prevalent in the eastern hemisphere. Many tribes and nations of old here in America had a spiritual life and religion quite different from our own today, though rather close to the ancient nature religions of the Old World. But they expressed a reverence for and understanding of all life that was outstanding and that we would be very wise to respect. It is time indeed to stop "strutting about like turkey cocks", as the Indians of Yucatan described the conduct of the first white men to visit them, and to learn a little humbleness and open our minds. Perhaps we might thus learn from the ancient peoples of America some things of vital importance to man's future existence.

chapter ONE

A Song Heard in the Dawn

"From the great rock I see it, the Daybreak Star, the sign of the dawning;
Above the mountain it rises and my heart dances.
Now the light comes, the light that makes me one with all life.
Like the tinamou I am, who sings in the dawn, who is humble with love,
Who walks in the circle of the greater love and the greater power.
Let me be like a ray of light, like a flower blazing with light,
Like the waterfall laughing with light, like the great tree also,
Mighty in its roots that split the rocks, mighty in its head that reaches the sky,
And its leaves catch the light and sing with the wind a song of the circle.

Let my life be like the rainbow, whose colors teach us unity;
Let me follow always the great circle, the roundness of power,
One with the moon and the sun, and the ripple of waters,
Following the sacred way of honor, a guide and protector to the weak,
A rock of strength in my word that shall say no evil, no lie nor deception.
Let me be like the otter, so loyal to his mate he will die for her,
So strong to his children they obey him as the shadows obey the sun;
And let me remember always the Great One, the Lord of the Dawning,
Whose Voice whispers to me in the breeze, whose words come to me out
Of all the circles of life, and whose command is like the thunder:
'Be kind, be kind, be brave, be brave, be pure, be pure,
Be humble as the earth, and be as radiant as the sunlight!' "

Rough translation of a Guaymi dawn song,
sung by Chio Jari

AS A VERY YOUNG MAN I was in the jungles of Panama and Costa Rica for two years, but on three different trips, collecting animals, plants, insects and other specimens for museums and private collectors. It was an amazing experience, filled with delight and adventure, but also with danger and foolishness, for I had much to learn. For a time I lived with an old jungle man, an American who had spent many years in Panama, and from him I learned some of the ways of the wilderness and some of the ways of being a man.

I was eighteen at the time I first knew him, and one great lesson I learned in the very first week I had come to live with him. Even at that early date I was awed by the fluid power with which he moved, the way he could chop down a tree with his great axe and make it fall so exactly as to hit a stake I had driven into the ground for him as a marker, and the silent command of his very presence when I walked with him in the jungle. Without saying a word he could convey to me that I must be silent, and I was!

One evening I was washing the dishes, and when I finished them I turned away from them to read a book I liked.

"Young man," he asked, "do you think you have finished those dishes?"

"Yes," I answered innocently.

He came close and examined my work. Then he moved a finger over a plate and it came off with a bit of food on it. He held this before my eyes and said with great emphasis:

"Listen closely! If you wish to stay with me, you will have to learn to do every job you do in the best way you can. This is not your best; you can do far better!"

The reproach in his eyes was like the strike of two steel swords. Without a word, I went back to the dishes and finished them as they should have been done. It was indeed a needed lesson, this understanding that every job was a challenge to the best within you. It was a lesson my parents had somehow been unable to teach me!

Later the two of us homesteaded a ranch in the high mountains of western Panama near the Costa Rican border. We called the place The Valley of the Clouds, but also Paradise Ranch or La Finca Paraisa, as the Panamanians say. I still remember with joy the hard work of building our own cabin out of the jungle, for out of the trees we created something strong and beautiful. We dug a pit and built above it a framework of small logs onto which we would roll the cut portion of a larger log about ten feet long and three feet thick. With our eleven-foot whip saw we trimmed four sides to make a rectangular block. Then Claude had me hold the black-inked string tight along one of the flat sides while by twanging the string he marked off the lines for the different boards we were to saw. Then, with me below and him above, we proceeded to saw out our own lumber, magnificent red-colored hardwood boards of the Pizarra tree that shone in the sunlight with a beautiful glow. These we used for the roof and sides of the cabin, but the floor Claude did by splitting logs with his great axe and trimming them flat.

We had to build a trail through wild jungle canyon country for sixteen miles, up and down the ridges. Over this trail we brought in food and supplies while we planted corn, beans, squash and other foods, plus a goodly number of young banana trees at the ranch. Behind our cabin a waterfall plunged and laughed and tinkled down the dark basalt cliffs, clustered with mosses and ferns, and to this we built a trestle on top of which we placed a trough made of split and half-hollowed logs. When finished it carried the crystal clear water of the mountain right by our kitchen window where we could dip it out with gourds or pans.

All about us was the thickness of plant and animal life, a myriad lush greenery and the whistling, warbling, grunting, sighing, growling, roaring, talking of jungle creatures. Every dawn our alarm clock was the tremendous roar of the howling monkeys, starting in distant treetops as a comparatively soft grunting "luk-luk-lukah-lukah-" and rising in crescendo till it seemed to shake the very mountains. Then might be heard, as the dawn strengthened, the "chak-lak-lak-lakah" of the chachalaca, a large turkeylike bird by the river, and the soft "teena-moooo" of the tinamous, or the baby-like scream of a sloth, hanging upside down like a mossy extension of some green jungle branch. But in the evening dimness more menacing sounds might be heard, such as the deep savage "uh-uh-uh-UH-UH-UH" of a great spotted cat, the jaguar, hunting down by the river. And always in the darkness sounded the whisper of padded feet, the sudden crashing sounds of a deer or tapir in the distance, or sounds of breaking branchlets in the jungle tops where coatimundis or kinkajous, striped ocelots or little spotted tiger cats might be roaming or hunting.

To the Valley of the Clouds and other parts of western Panama and southern Costa Rica I came on three different journeys, always with the love of the high jungle growing in my heart.

Three times I had Indian boys helping collect specimens, but in the first two instances they were tame Indians of the lowlands, their people conquered by the Spaniards. First was Lalio, really a mestizo, part Indian, a good worker and fine companion until his sophisticated older brother came up from the lowland cities with the idea that a person should work as little as possible for as much money as possible! In a week I reluctantly had to let Lalio go. The second boy, Francisco, lasted only two weeks, as he too was steeped in the idea of working very little for great wages!

Soon after this I visited an old man who had traveled far and lived long among many of the Indian peoples of Central America. He had twinkling eyes in a brown face, deeply lined with wrinkles; his eyes laughed even more when he heard the story of those first two boys.

"Leave the tame Indians alone," he exclaimed. "They have been spoiled by the white man and forgotten the good ways of old. Find a mountain Guaymi of the Serrania de Tabasara, the wild mountains northeast of here. They still walk with honor. A young man of this people will be the best you can find!"

How I found Chio Jari, the wild Guaymi of the mountains, is a story too long to be given here, but he came to me far more as a friend than as one who works for only a wage. True I paid him five dollars a month and board and room, which he considered a princely sum, but money was of less interest to him than experience; and soon he was as close to me and as useful as my right hand! Stocky and strong, with a round moonlike face, he walked through the forest with the quietness of mist and the sureness of an accomplished jungle man, all at the age of seventeen. I had to teach him Spanish as he understood only a little of it, and my English would have done him no good in Panama.

Like his people, he used to laugh a lot. One time he was taking a bath down at the river and I knew he not only loved to soap himself, but was in danger of using up a whole bar of soap in one bath if I let him! So I shouted several times that morning for him to come up to the cabin and get to work. No answer, just a lot of splashing! When he did arrive I had seldom seen a cleaner boy!

Standing akimbo and staring at him fiercely, I demanded: "Chio, why did you not come when I shouted for you?"

He looked me innocently in the eyes and declared: "I could not hear you, Senor."

"Chio, don't you lie to me. You could hear me easily!"

Now he stood up very straight and tall. "We Guaymi do not lie!" Then he paused a moment dramatically and said: "Everytime you started to shout I just ducked my head under water!" Whereupon he burst into a laugh that fairly shook the jungle. And I could not help laughing too.

Another story about Chio demonstrates not only his tremendous humor, but something more important. We used to go on long exploring hikes to different areas and sometimes we would arrive back at our cabin in the mountains after dark. Walking down the trail behind him, for it was he who seemed to have eyes to see in the dark, I could not help being nervous at strange sounds that often came out of the jungle, such as the snap of a twig breaking, a weird grunt or coughing, or a slithering sound among the leaves. I tried to hide this from him, but I knew he knew how I felt. In the dark one evening, as we were nearing home he exclaimed: "The tame people of the lowlands are afraid of the jaguars and the big snakes, but we of the mountains walk through the dark like warriors. We do not send out the smell of fear, and they, the people of the night, leave us alone!"

We had only gone a little farther, walking silently, when suddenly he burst into a run down the jungle trail toward the river, leaving me completely alone!

I was tempted to yell for him to come back, but after what he had just said, I knew he was testing me, so I grabbed at the shreds of my courage, gritted my teeth and did not shout. But now the world of darkness seemed to take on a deepening menace, and I had the creepy feeling that many eyes were watching me. I wanted to run, but knew I would probably trip and fall if I did, so I tried to walk as quietly as possible.

Suddenly a deep grunting sounded by the river and I very nearly took a twenty foot broad jump down the trail until I realized it was the cry of a tapir, a large dark cowlike animal with a short trunk that relates it to the elepant. I knew that tapirs were harmless to man in most cases, and was just congratulating myself that all was well and I was getting near home, when I unexpectedly tripped on something in the trail and the next instant felt something fall from the great tree above me with a loud "swoosh!" Thick rope-like coils wrapped themselves around me and I was nightmarishly sure I had been attacked by a large snake!

My yelling must have been heard a half mile away as I tried desperately to fight myself free of the thing that clung to me. Suddenly, almost without realizing it, I broke loose from my attacker and rushed off down the trail. As I splashed through the river, however, a minute later, I became aware of two things: first that I had escaped from that "snake" very easily; and secondly, that somebody up at the cabin was laughing uproariously! Grimly I stopped running and settled down to a walk.

When I reached the cabin I found Chio rolling on the ground, almost helpless with laughter. He had one of our lanterns lit and in its light I could see the tears streaming down his round brown face. Not feeling very humorous, myself, I began to shake him. Finally he calmed down enough to grab the lantern and beckon me to follow him. We went down the trail together, crossed the river and within a few minutes came to where I had been "attacked."

There was my "snake!" It was a huge vine that Chio had cleverly set in the tree above the trail, using a smaller vine to trip the larger one into falling on me when I came along!

He began to shake again with laughter, but there was no condemnation nor sneer in his laughter, only tremendous good humor, and I finally began to laugh ruefully with him. Oddly enough my fear of the jungle darkness began to go away from me from that moment. As another Indian once told me: "Snake does not bite man; snake bites what man thinks!"

Not long after this came one of the most tremendous experiences of my life. I had long noticed Chio Jari's wonderful loyalty and his absolute trustworthiness and honesty. When he did a job, he always did it better than you expected and was always eager to learn. Many necessary jobs around the ranch he did without even being asked to do them, just because he saw they needed to be done. On top of all this he was relaxed in a most extraordinary way, so that just being around him encouraged a calm and happy feeling. I occasionally wondered how this could be developed in such a young man, but did not really begin to ask questions until the strange event happened. In fact until this new happening, I felt so at ease with Chio and felt such a joy at having him as a companion that I began to take him for granted. It had really not occurred to me yet to ask why he was so extraordinarily different from other young men and boys I knew.

One morning I woke up in the very beginning of the dawn, a time considerably before the monkeys would start their great howlings and roarings that woke the rest of the jungle. Chio and I slept on two crude bunks up under the roof of our cabin, about twelve feet off the ground. As in other dawns when I had awakened early, I saw that he was gone from his bunk. Other times I had been too sleepy or lazy to follow him, but this morning something drove me to rise from my bunk and go seeking him.

I moved as quietly as possible out from the cabin and through the trail that led by the high cornstalks of our clearing and under the banana trees to the east where a waterfall tossed down the rocks of the great cliff. Somehow I knew that was where he would be and suddenly I came around a curve of the trail and saw him. I stopped and stood perfectly still as if struck and paralyzed by a bolt of lightning. But the blow that struck me was not material, it was a blow of the spirit. To understand what happened to me that early dawn with the first dim light beginning to suffuse the dark jungle and glisten on the water falling over the cliff, you must know that at that period in my life I considered myself an atheist. I was being trained in anthropology and biology at the University of California and had become fascinated with the scientific method. This method teaches the scientist to have an open mind to everything he investigates, but strangely enough, though I was indeed trying to follow this open mind in my study of the material world, I had completely closed my mind to the spiritual world. I had come to regard all religion as a lot of fairy stories, too dogmatic and filled with superstitions to be worthy of the attention of an intelligent man.

Now I saw Chio Jari standing on a great rock on the edge of the jungle, his arms lifted to the sky and his body—indeed his whole being —suffused with a strange power. He was singing a song whose words I did not understand, a dawn song, and yet one whose feeling was so beautiful and wonderful that I sensed with overwhelming comprehension that somehow a spirit was pouring from him into the sky to meet a greater spirit above. Indeed, as I watched him that morning completely enthralled, he seemed to grow into a being from another world, sacred and divine, whose voice and body became a part of all creation. As the sunlight began to come and the jungle awaken, he seemed to be literally bringing into being that golden light that touched first the high jungle beyond the cliffs and then reached down into the river canyon to finally light the river itself first to silver, and then to gold. As bird song after bird song sounded from the trees, his voice joined them in praise of the glory of the dawn. As the howling monkeys burst forth with their "luk-luk-lukah-lukah—!" that rose in a frenzy of worship also to the coming of day, Chio's song faded away, but the power of it would be always remembered within me. For the first time in my life I became aware that spirit existed. My days as an atheist were ended forever, though my trail to the spirit would be yet a long and hard one with many ups-and-downs.

The last time I saw Chio before returning to the United States to continue my education was one of those extraordinarily beautiful evenings that come occasionally to the jungle mountains. The air was balmy and warm, but not hot; the moon was gloriously full and like a great yellow ball in the east; the river was rustling and gurgling by us where we sat quietly talking, and the moonbeams glistened on its waters. But all about us in the jungle night, the trees and bushes were alive with myriad lights, as if we were in a fairy forest. It was one of those great dance times of the insect peoples, when the fireflies, the lantern flies and the cuculla click beetles, with their small green headlights and their great bright flashing red taillights, were dancing all about us.

I was trying to get out of Chio something about his religion that night, but he was very shy to talk about such things. I was pressing him, however, because I very much wanted to know. That earlier dawn-time I had become aware that somehow he had in his life something of far greater power and value than anything I had in mine. All my material possessions and my good home and parents in the United States, all my sophisticated education and all the increase of it I might get in the years ahead I knew was nothing compared to what he had! Yet he was not a Christian, and unlike some religious people I had known, he had none of the "holier than thou" attitude that had so repelled me from religion at an earlier time in my life. He was indeed like a simple and beautiful child, who had somehow maintained that simple beauty and goodness and yet grown into a wise youth. It reminded me of a saying of Jesus that I had never understood before, where He says: "Save ye become as little children, ye cannot enter the Kingdom of Heaven." Chiro Jari, I saw, had maintained the simplicity and purity of the child and developed the strength and wisdom of the man. His life was indeed like flowing water, in which there were no hangups of pride, vanity nor dogmatism, and yet in which a high honor and a high moral standard became as natural as the flow of blood and as relaxed and beautiful as the singing of birds.

Finally, when I urged him that I was leaving in the morning and would probably never see him again, he answered my queries by pointing with his finger to the moon and making a circle. Then he made another circle which he indicated meant the sun. He pointed also around the whole rim of the sky and earth and told me this meant both sky and earth. His finger outlined the curves of the leaves of the trees, and he indicated the curving movements of the ripples and waves in the river as it moved over the rocks. Then he spoke and a thrill of power came with his words:

"All beautiful things form circles or curves," he said, "and the rainbow is half a circle of colors in harmony as a sign from the Grandfather in the Sky that we must complete the circle by making our lives as fine as the rainbow. If we sing the song of the circle every dawn, as the old ones teach us, and at other times during the day and night, then this is the way we must live as the Grandfather wants us to live."

He would speak no more, but down through the years I have come to understand that Chio Jari was a man in the full and beautiful sense of the word, one who had the teachings of the Great Spirit sung into his very blood and bone until a lie or other unworthy deed would be as impossible for him as to cut off his finger with an axe! I shall always be searching to find and understand more deeply the inner meanings of his story. It is a search I believe could be most rewarding.

chapter TWO

The Spirit Behind Native American Religions

The rhythm of the night and the rhythm of the day are obviously different. To the American Indian the spectacular drama of the dawn and the sunset, each with their streaming clouds of glory, when dark and light change guard, has a definite effect on his physical, mental and spiritual attitude. His personal life, as well as that of his tribe, is in tune with the infinite when he prays with ceremony at the dawn and again at nightfall. Strongly aided by the prophetic dreams and visions of the Wise Old Ones, his religion and belief in life both here and hereafter, as well as his personal life, are all paralleled by the rhythms of the day and night and of the seasons. Daytime symbolizes physical life for the conscious mind and body, and night time symbolizes sleep and death of the conscious mind. Here the vital activity of the unconscious, or the dream pattern, is given freedom. This mysterious spirit of the soul of the individual is the real life and the real self, which is no longer under the restrictions and limitations of the physical body.

From *Tapestries in Sand,* by David Villasenor,
Naturegraph Publishers, 1963

I HAVE LONG BEEN INTERESTED in the religions of the Native Americans, but after commencing an intensive study of these religions two years ago, I am convinced they are far too complex and varied to fit as yet into neat categories. In fact, it may be very difficult ever to do this for three reasons. First, scientific study of these religions started only in very recent years. A tremendous lot of information has been lost due to the dying off of so many of the old people who still had some knowledge of them. Second, the ethnologists and other scientists who have studied these religions have been of many varied backgrounds, themselves, hence their interpretations of this very complex and subjectively difficult subject have often clashed. Third, the Indian informants, themselves, often differ in their interpretations and their ideas, and some even changed their own ideas over a comparatively short period of time. For example, when I was visiting the Museum of Navajo Ceremonial Art at Santa Fe, New Mexico a few years ago, a friendly curator told me that they had asked one old Navajo Medicine Man to explain the meaning of a sandpainting he had done for them. He did so, but the trouble was he also came back to the museum twice later, each time giving a completely new interpretation of the same sandpainting!

We would be wise therefore not to come to any dogmatic conclusions about American Indian religions. What intensive study does show is that there are certain patterns of thought, plan, organization and spirit that begin to emerge from the confusion. If we can sort these out and study them carefully, we can begin to establish some tentative rules as to how these religions evolved and perhaps better understand their roots and functions. But we need to be careful not to make the mistakes of the early students of this subject who labeled practically all early religions of the Americas "primitive" or "simple". Oddly enough, even people who have a very simple culture with the crudest type dwellings or tools, as did the Australian Aboriginals before white contact, may still have an extremely complex religion. And we must shy away from such words as "savages" or "barbarians", especially because these names have been used in the past to justify white treatment of the Native Americans. In past centuries many whites assumed that if you could call an Indian a savage this gave you the right to enslave him or put him on a reservation or treat him in some other way as an inferior to be manipulated and trained to change his outlook to that of his conquerors. But who has a right to judge who is inferior or superior? The Indian was often far more in tune with his environment and understood it much better than the whites who conquered him, and many Indian societies were almost completely free of crime, a condition lamentably lacking in most European societies at the time of the conquest.

Ecologic and economic basis of religion in America

Since there were no flock-driving nomads in America, such as were and still are so well-known in European and Asiatic areas, the two great divisions ecologically and economically in America were between those who were hunters and those who were cultivators of crops. Of course there were many tribes who stood in between these major divisions, having some elements of both, as for example, the Pawnees, who lived in earth lodges about half of the year and raised corn, beans and squash, but spent most of the rest of the year hunting buffalo and other game.

The religion of the pure hunters was usually the simplest of all, with some tribes such as the Athabaskans of northern Canada in the west and the Algonquins of northern Canada in the northeast having each individual hunter practically acting as his own medicine man and priest. Each individual in such a case sought for his own vision and medicine power with which to ward off dangerous spirits. This pattern was also found among the simple desert tribes of the Great Basin, such as the Paiutes and Western Shoshones, and of similar hunting tribes of the northeastern part of Mexico. To them the world was occupied with many dangerous spirits and avoiding their evil influence was more important usually than any concept embodying sky gods or a higher being.

There were, however, a number of pure hunting tribes, who had once been agriculturists, but who had reverted to hunting when the horse came to America with the Spaniards and gave these tribes greater mobility and the ability to hunt the vast buffalo herds of the western plains. These tribes, such as the Sioux, had a much more socially differentiated and specialized religion in which priests and medicine men had a dominant part, and in which sky gods and even one Great Spirit, who was manifest in all other things, were recognized and worshipped. It was some of these tribes that picked up very noble thoughts about religions as furnished to them by culture heroes, as we shall see later. It is these people whose search for visions we know most about, and who, I believe, sometimes reached the highest levels of nobility and altruism in such searches.

The mixed hunting and agriculture tribes, such as the Pawnees, Iroquois and Osage, had a religion in general similar to that of the hunting tribes that had once been agricultural, with the difference that several purely agricultural ceremonies and dieties are to be found among them. Thus great seasonal ceremonies at times of planting and times of harvesting are found among these tribes. Where a culture hero comes into the picture, as is the case with Degandawidah of the Iroquois, he usually purifies the religion of the past and brings in higher concepts of morals and of cooperation between peoples. Many young men of these tribes used to go on vision searches to strengthen their spirit.

Among the plateau hunting and gathering tribes such as the Yakima, Nez Perce and Umatilla of the interior northwest, dreamer women often took almost equal rank with the men visionaries as leaders of the religion of the tribe. These peoples often have legends of a "changer" or a human being who came and changed things for the better, including the religion, but it is not always clear whether he was a real culture hero or not. However, the high moral standards prevalent among these tribes in the pre-white times gives some evidence of a culture hero in their past.

While the tribes of the northwest coast area, from the Hoopa and Yurok of northwestern California to the Tlingit of southern Alaska, were also hunting and fishing and gathering people, without agriculture, the tremendous plenitude and richness of the fish crop, particularly salmon, gave them much leisure time. Consequently they developed elaborate religious ceremonies, but their emphasis on personal wealth and the power and prestige stemming from wealth made their religion rather individualistic. Both women and men sought spiritual and healing powers as doctors and usually went on vision searches to get them, but the bulk of the population depended for prestige on their relationships to wealthy families. The vision seekers often deliberately sought spiritual power for the purpose of gathering wealth so the end desired was a personal family one. Their legends emphasized battles against monsters, and stories of a trickster called Raven, who took the place of the Coyote trickster most of the other western tribes had. I have found no sign of a definite culture hero among these tribes. In most of these tribes visions or dreams came most to the wealthy.

The increasing amount of leisure that intensified agriculture brings to people became evident in what is now the southeastern states around fifteen hundred years ago and spread up through the Mississippi and Ohio Valleys with the Mound-builder culture of A.D. 200 to 1400. Evidence from the great mounds that were built throughout the area shows a long peaceful era with much trading and cultural exchange and the development of elaborate religious ceremonies, all possibly due to a culture hero who either came to the area or sent disciples up out of Mexico. Long peaceful cooperation like this certainly is most likely to come from a strong religious impulse which unites peoples and breaks down walls between them. After the Mound-builder culture fell, the tribes turned strongly to war again and even to human sacrifice and tyrannical petty kings. This only serves to emphasize the long time of peace and spiritual uplift that preceded it. The priesthood that developed during the time of peace may have been a fulltime profession, but in more recent time priests of such southeastern tribes as the Creeks and the Choctaws were part-time professionals, working at other jobs during part of each week. Most young men of this area sought for visions and spirit power, as in the forest tribes of the northeast.

The southwestern pueblo peoples made of religion something still more elaborate, spending almost all their spare time aside from necessary work at the various ceremonies. Their life, in fact, was almost all one huge religious ceremony, but the deep sincerity and intense spirituality of every move in the ceremonies and in their preparation cannot be denied. The ceremonies were mostly directed toward having good crops. The direct vision search was largely unknown among the Pueblo tribes whose agricultural and rain-producing ceremonies had largely supplanted it, but dreams were considered important and often were interpreted with keen interest as to their meaning and what the recipient should do. The priests, as in the Southeast, were semi-professionals, working in the fields with the crops when they were not directing ceremonies. There was a long peaceful period in the Southwest among the pueblo peoples similar to that in the Mississippi Valley, but this appears to have been broken both by increasing quarrels among the pueblos and the coming of warlike hunting tribes, such as the Navajos and the Apaches, out of the north, and the Comanches and Kiowas out of the east. A legend of the Hopis tells of the time their ancestors were in the cliff-dwellings of Mesa Verde and how the final abandonment of these ancient villages came because of a quarrel between two powerful religious factions that caused a terrible drouth.

In Mexico and Guatemala the great civilizations of the Maya and of Teotihuacan had their beginnings about 200 B.C. These people developed agriculture to a point where a leisure class of nobility could develop as well as professional priests, artisans, merchants, and even mathematicians and astronomers. The very long era of peace, cooperation and trading back and forth between and among these cultures, which lasted till around A.D. 750 to 800, is proof to me of a strong religious impulse that taught cooperation between human groups. There is strong evidence that the Mexican culture and possibly the empire of Teotihuacan, as well as the great southern lowland Mayan cities of Tikal, Copan, Palenque and so forth, collapsed into a century or more of confusion and barbarism mainly due to a breakdown of social structure from within, rather than from outside invasions, even though Teotihuacan was sacked by invaders from the north about A.D. 750. The illustrations on the walls of Mayan cities that can be dated towards the end of the first grand period of Mayan civilization shows both nobles and priests acting with cruelty and arrogance towards other Mayans, presumably those of the lower classes or captives from other Mayan cities or both. This strongly suggests a breakdown of the religion in which it ceased to be a means for bringing cooperation and kindness between people and degenerated into an instrument of power for the ruling classes. If so it shows good reason for a breakdown as the lower class people more and more sullenly refused to cooperate or even rose in outright revolt or fled in fear and anger away from the cities. This contribution of the collapse of the religion to the general collapse of the culture, which of course includes a number of other contributing factors, seems to have been largely ignored or played down by most archaelogists.

More on these great civilizations and what happened to them will be explained in Chapter Nine. Suffice to say here that the newer cultures of the Toltecs, Aztecs and the later Mayas of the League of Mayapan in northern Yucatan, which developed in the half-thousand years before the coming of the Spaniards, saw a priesthood closely connected with a warrior nobility and a series of kings. The priests in the beginning of this latter era, under the influence of the great prophet-king of Tula (the Toltec capital), Quetzalcoatl (The Feathered Serpent), were generally setting high standards of morals as well as kindness and cooperation between peoples. Though the moral standards remained surprisingly high right up to the time of the Spanish conquest, much of the priesthood degenerated in time into instruments for the conquest of other people and the blood-bath of human sacrifice in the name of the war gods. Actually, human sacrifice in the great Aztec temples was supposed to have been for the purpose of keeping the sun burning and supplying light and heat to the world. Another main function of the priesthood, or for at least large portions of them, was the same as that of the priests of the religion of the pueblo tribes to the north, to keep the rains falling at the right times to encourage growth of the crops. Other priests acted as teachers to the young, particularly in the field of morals. Visions generally were sought by the priests and healers.

In South America, among the Aymara and Quechua peoples of the Inca Empire, the priesthood was closely intertwined with the sacred Inca ruling class, who worshipped the sun as the chief manifestation of the Great Spirit. These people also, as had the Chibchas of Columbia and other more civilized nations of South and Central America, developed a highly successful agriculture and, with the Incas, even developed the use of burden carrying animals, the llamas. But most of them did not have the writing with pictographs and hieroglyphics that had been developed by the Maya and the Mexicans, nor proficiencies with mathematics and astronomy. The priesthood of the Incas, however, had not only kept a high moral standard, but developed methods of cooperation and understanding between peoples in the Inca Empire on a very high order, with surprisingly little human sacrifice and other destructive cruelties. They too had had a great culture hero, Viracocha, who taught them noble standards of character (see Chapter Ten). Vision seeking was mostly a privilege of priests and healers.

The Indians of California, outside of the northwest tribes who partook of the northwest coast culture, and the tribes along the Colorado River, had a remarkably similar culture, but some interesting variations in religion. Most of them were hunters and gatherers, but the presence of fine crops of acorns from the oak trees prevalent in most of this area, gave them such a steady source of nutritious food that gathering plant food outweighed hunting in their economy and gave them something almost like an agricultural base. Among the mountain tribes and those in other outlying areas such as the desert fringe this source of food was not ample enough to allow much leisure time. They therefore tended to keep their religions simple and based mainly on the curing of ills and the teaching of conduct by the shamans and chiefs. With these more primitive tribes evil spirits and ghosts were inclined to dominate the religions, with the shamans acting as guards against these frightening beings or sometimes using their evil power to blackmail or destroy those they wished to control or did not like.

In the great valleys, however, where the rivers flowed and the acorns were thick, elaborate ceremonial-type religions developed and there were priests as well as shamans. The two main religious movements or cults were the Kuksu cult in the north, which had great curing and moral-teaching ceremonies each year, and the jimsonweed cult of the southern California Indians, which involved the distinctive ceremony of having the young people seek visions by drinking a hallucination-producing beverage made from jimson weed, thornapple, or datura, as it is variously called. The culture heroes of these peoples are described in Chapter Ten. Among most of the California Indians it was the medicine men and women and their initiates who sought visions.

**The shamans or medicine men
and the priests of Native American religions**

It is rather painful to use either the word "shaman" or "medicine man" to describe general types of Native American religious leaders because these two words tend to give the impression of a witch doctor—a man or woman who uses powers of magic and sleight of hand as well as calling up dark spirits to aid in his or her control over people. Also these words never give the idea of the great numbers of different types of specialists among medicine men, some healing sprains and fractures of limbs, others specializing in certain diseases, still others acting as psychotherapists or moral or spiritual persuaders, and some covering, among the more isolated mountain or desert tribes, all these professions in one person.

Also the quality and kind of influence possessed by the medicine men may vary greatly through different shades between good and evil. Some tribes, such as the Yuki of the northern California mountains, were literally terrorized by shamans or medicine men who used their powers to control and use the people for selfish ends. Other tribes, such as the Cheyennes and the Sioux, had medicine men who could actually be called holy men because they were so dedicated to service to their people without thought of any material gain and who helped maintain the highest standards of cooperation, honor and chastity. These men were almost invariably the products of the influence of a great culture hero, such as some of those described in later chapters.

In most tribes the shamans or medicine men and women usually varied between the more selfish kinds and the more altruistic. Most of them as children were often more sensitive than usual and often with psychological or physical problems or abilities that particularly leaned them towards the shamans professions, often having more vivid dreams than other people. Some even had great physical handicaps, such as epilepsy or other brain defects that caused them to go into trances or fits, which to the superstitious people about them seemed proof they were possessed by spirits. Others were particularly clever at sleight-of-hand or other magical tricks by which they could fool the common people. Whatever the cause, their potential ability was often spotted by older medicine men or women and they were taken in hand and trained for the job.

Being human and subject to influences both good and bad, some moved more one way than the other. In many tribes good shamans were in constant demand to save people from the evil magic and poisoning efforts of bad shamans. In fact, in such tribes it could often be claimed with fair accuracy that certain sicknesses were caused by bad shamans.

If, for example, one is persuaded—as often happened among these people—that a bad shaman has obtained one's discarded nail clippings and has cast a spell over them to kill him, he is likely to die just purely from the auto-suggestion unless he can find a good shaman to break the spell.

The priest illustrates the same wide spectrum of behavior from good to evil. If he used his ceremonies to help and strengthen people in good deeds, then he is obviously following the will and teachings of the Great Spirit as given through such founders of religion as the prophets and culture heroes. But if he uses ceremonies and the natural control over the people because of his supposed holiness and power for selfish ends to control, manipulate and frighten others, then he is working in the service of the evil principle in life, caused mainly by self-indulgence.

Since most humans beings are naturally selfish, the whole history of religion in America would probably be very dark indeed if it were not for the coming of the shining beings we call prophets or culture heroes. Whether they should be called Prophets with a capital P or just prophets or culture heroes is unimportant. What is important is that they directed the vision search of the Native Americans to their greatest heights and inspired beautiful and unselfish hearts that made some parts of ancient America and some long periods of its history true paradises of human cooperation and love. It is they who most strongly brought to the American Indians those qualities of closeness and harmony with nature and with each other that made them great and from which other peoples should learn. They and those who have learned to reflect their goodness and wisdom are the true Voices of Earth and Sky referred to in this book!

————

The search for a vision through the use of hallucinogenic drugs, such as peyote, thornapple and the sacred mushrooms of some of the Mexican Indians is outside the scope of this book. When used under careful ceremonial conditions with a religion of high moral standards such as the Native American Church and its peyote, they may indeed have value, particularly in overcoming alcoholism. But this may be similar to the value of a crutch when there is a broken leg. When the leg is well the crutch is no longer needed. A vision search through training and preparation of the mind and a vision vigil in which concentration on the spirit is total would likely be more effective in the long run. (Good books on the effects and uses of these various drugs in the vision search are given in the bibliography.)

chapter THREE

Learning from Mistakes

DARKNESS SONG

We wait in the darkness!
Come, all ye who listen,
Help in our night journey;
Now no sun is shining;
Now no star is glowing;
Come, show us the pathway;
The night is not friendly;
She closes her eyelids;
The moon has forgotten us,
We wait in the darkness!

From the Iroquois, as translated by Harriet M. Converse, in *Myths and Legends of the United States Iroquois,* edited by Arthur C. Parker; N.Y. State Mus. Bulletin, December 25, 1908. Reprinted in *The Sky Clears,* by A. Grove Day, Univ. of Nebraska Press, 1951.

THE WHITE PEOPLE HAVE MADE innumerable mistakes in dealing with the native peoples of America and their lack of understanding has been incredible. Yet the Native Americans, on their side, have also made numerous mistakes too, all of which has created a gulf of prejudice and misunderstanding between the two peoples that is very sad. It is time now for both peoples to learn from their mistakes, to grow in the spirit and come together in understanding.

There is a fundamental psychological blindness that infects most all nations and tribes of the earth and which makes each group continue to look at others just through the one channel of their own particular background, a very narrow view indeed! Thus they continue to exalt their own culture and people in their minds and look down on or be afraid of or hate other people without trying to understand them. A secondary psychological blindness appears when a people are severely conquered by another people, as happened to most Indian tribes. The traumatic experience, especially on sensitive children, is so great that these children are cowed into believing that their conquerors are much superior people. This belief may be reinforced by the way they came to be taught in the schools of those who conquered them. Convinced they are inferior, they continue to act as inferiors even though they usually have quite equal mental and physical abilities. But their inferiority complex and the darkness of the prejudices with which they are surrounded inhibits their efforts to grow mentally and spiritually, often with disastrous effects.

A startling example of this came to my attention at an Indian school I visited some years ago. This school, meant for Indian children only, was supervised and taught primarily by whites. The white attitude towards these children was often, at least subconsciously if not consciously, that they were very hard to teach because of an inherent lack of ability. There was little understanding of the terrible loss these children had suffered upon being deprived of their culture and language, or the other traumatic experiences of sensitive Indian children in a white world.

One class at the school was considered almost completely hopeless, the whole group thought of as being, at best, only on the level of morons. Fortunately a young teacher from Oklahoma came to the school who was part Indian. He asked to have this class, even though warned that they were beyond hope. He at first did find them sullen, silent and uncooperative, but he understood what the other teachers had not—that these children, badly hurt by white misunderstanding, had withdrawn within themselves, forming a protective coating or armor of apparent stupidity around their true selves.

For the first few months with these students he made little attempt to give them any formal teaching. Instead he took thom on walks and hikes, visits to places of interest, and told them stories and legends of his Indian ancestors and theirs, showing always a great friendliness and kindness, though also firmness. Gradually their hearts and minds began to open, until one by one they began to find themselves learning many new things and enjoying it. Soon the whole class took a great leap forward, as their faces opened with smiles and laughter and their eyes, so long dark, sad and hidden, began to sparkle with interest. So also will a whole Native American people come alive and renew their natural abilities and genius when relieved of the darkness of misunderstanding and prejudice that still surrounds them.

A third type of psychological blindness appears when some among the conquered people begin to snap back after the defeat and realize that they are really a great people, and that their conquerors have many weaknesses and have done a lot of injustices to them. At such a point they may form movements that reflect hate and prejudice towards the whites, forgetting that true greatness is based on deeds and thoughts of creativity, understanding and love. Thus they repeat the same mistakes of the whites, for prejudice from either side is self-defeating, as the old wise ones of their own people often warned them not to do.

I once came to an Apache reservation in the Southwest with an Indian friend and met a dynamic young medicine man. He showed signs of greatness in the keen look of his eyes and the proud way he held his head, but unfortunately he took the downward path of degrading the white people. For some time he would speak only to my companion —not to me—but at last he looked at me with a sly glance, and said: "The white people are just a bunch of flies and should all be swatted!"

I did not argue with him, but agreed that the white people had done a lot of bad things to the Indians because of prejudice and lack of understanding, but that I was doing my best to teach them how really wonderful the Indians were. At this he suddenly began to weep for his people and all their greatness lost and bemoaned the evils that had happened to them. Then suddenly he changed and began to boast about what great warriors the Apaches were. He told with considerable relish how they had bested other tribes such as the pueblo peoples, treating them brutally, and how they had won many battles against the Mexicans in the old days; they had even enslaved many Mexicans. He did not seem to realize that in speaking of the Apache treatment of the Mexicans and pueblos he was showing how white Americans had actually followed the Apache footsteps in their treatment of other peoples!

This story shows in effect how we are most of us too human—human in the sense of our flaws and our mistakes, our smallness and our cruelty, rather than in our capacity for greatness. Some white people, in their revulsion against what other whites have done in the past to Indians, may romanticize too much about our Native Americans, making them appear nobler than they really are, and hiding their eyes to any weaknesses. But the truth is almost universal that to be human is to make mistakes, and some mistakes of all races are pretty terrible!

Actually the ease with which the whites conquered the Indians, who in most cases were superior fighting men from their long training in hunting and wilderness living, was not due nearly so much to superior white weapons nor to diseases, as many believe, as it was to the lack of cooperation and outright hostility between the Indian tribes themselves. Thus the cruelty and arrogance of the Aztecs of Mexico towards other Mexican nations caused many of these other peoples to join the Spaniards in the conquest of the Aztecs. The League of the Iroquois Five Nations, who were justly proud of their fine organization and warlike ability, unwisely used these two qualities to crush most brutally tribe after tribe in the East and Midwest which might have been their allies against the whites. When it was the Iroquois' turn to be hurt, as they were most badly by Sullivan's army in the Mohawk Valley in 1780, they spoke in righteous horror against the whites, forgetting that they had used exactly the same tactics in previous centuries against other Native Americans! But their greatest forgetting was of the wise teachings of their own great culture heroes (see Chapter Six), Degandawidah and Hiawatha, who had counseled them to use peaceful methods to bring all the Indians together. In Alaska the closely kinned Aleuts and Eskimos have hated each other for centuries, as have the two great Indian nations of the Haida and the Tlingits. Only recently have some of them begun to get together in friendship.

It is time indeed for all races to grow in wisdom and understanding, to see the enormity and foolishness of past mistakes, while going on to true greatness, which means to begin more and more to understand each other, help each other and establish the highest ideals of cooperation and conduct. The Indians are beginning to learn the technical and educational know-how and wisdom of the white people. They are also trying in a beginning way to preserve and enhance the best in their cultural past, but the white people need even more help from the Indians on how to achieve a sense of harmony with earth and sky and all living things so this earth, this beautiful green and glowing earth, can be returned to its former beauty and be spared from pollution and over-exploitation. And both need to build again the honor and purity of conduct that is taught in the lives of the truly fine and spiritual human beings of all races. Part of this upward path means putting behind the immaturities of prejudice and faulty pride and working instead to bring equality, justice and understanding to all.

Though American anthropologists, as they probably will readily admit, have made serious mistakes in dealing with the Native Americans and have lost some golden opportunities to learn more about their past culture, and particularly their religions, they have also been among the first white people to seek to renew this culture and to understand it. On the whole their service to the Indians by helping preserve knowledge of the old cultures and working to break down the prejudices of other whites has been much greater than their disservice which has largely come about from prying too clumsily and with too little sensitivity and courtesy into Indian minds and life. There are signs today that they are realizing past mistakes and are having a more sensitive and understanding approach, particularly in the field of religion, which too often in the past has been treated as a curiosity or a superstition.

Some of the first breakthroughs in reaching a sensitive understanding of Indian minds and spiritual power came fairly early. For example, Drs. Kroeber and Waterman of the University of California at Berkeley were fortunate enough to become intimately acquainted with the life and thoughts of Ishi, the last of the free Indians of California who came down out of the mountains near Mt. Lassen in 1911 and gave himself up to the whites. They were astonished, as were many other educated whites of the time who met Ishi, at his extraordinary natural courtesy and the high honor of his conduct as well as his very spiritual nature and intimate love of nature. Yet he was a Yahi, of a tribe that in the 1850's had been blasted time and again in the newspapers as cruel and ruthless savages. The newspapers, of course, had not known or had ignored the fact that Ishi's people had been driven in desperation to strike back at the whites due to the ruthless. way the whites treated them and took away their land.

When Ishi was taken back to his native territory of Deer Creek Canyon in the Sierras to show the scientists how he had lived in the old days, they became aware of the very deep feeling he had for different places in the canyon, a feeling far more widespread than most white people have for the land about them and the life in it. In fact, Ishi was almost overwhelmed with sadness many times and his new friends had to work hard to keep him cheered-up. This feeling we now can have from the fine book, *Ishi In Two Worlds,* which makes plain the complex and wonderful nature of a human being of another race, Ishi of the Yahi. We need to apply this sort of insight toward all the Native Americans to see in them the same potential greatness.

Two other examples of sensitivity and real understanding of the Indian mind and religion are to be found in two other excellent books, though about the same person, Black Elk, holy man of the Oglala Sioux. One is by John Neihhardt, called *Black Elk Speaks,* and the other was edited by Joseph Eppes Brown, an ethnologist, and called *The Sacred Pipe.* Both books show in great detail the marvelous closeness of a great Indian to all living things, and his overwhelming sensitivity to and understanding of the holiness of human life when lived in harmony with the Great Spirit.

Another man, who even earlier than all the others saw the true greatness and meaning of the Indian religions, was Hartley Burr Alexander, philosopher, poet and anthropologist, whose book, *The World's Rim, Great Mysteries of the American Indians,* is a classic of in-depth understanding of a great people. I can think also of several other sensitive anthropologists, including Dr. C. Hart Merriam in California, and Dr. Gladys Reichard, with her fine book on *Navajo Religion* and, more recently, Carlos Castaneda, with his frank books on Don Juan, the Yaqui medicine man. These writers have all worked diligently toward better understanding of a wonderful race.

While taking courses in anthropology at the University of California at Berkeley in 1936-37-38, I listened in awe to the lectures of the great anthropologists, such as Drs. Lowie and Kroeber, but my baptism of working under an anthropologist directly with Indians came in the summer of 1937. At that time I went with a graduate anthropology student, Harold Driver, later Dr. Harold Driver, to record some of the culture of the Indian tribes on the Hoopa Reservation in northwestern California. Here, studying the Hoopa, Yurok, Karok, and Chilula, I was inevitably led by my own blindness to make some of the mistakes I saw later must have flawed the work of many anthropologists.

In those days the tape recorder, the present most usual and sometimes useful tool of the anthropologist, was not available so we took copious notes on the ancient culture while listening to many of the oldest inhabitants of the valley. Often this had to be done through an interpreter, which I realized later probably doubled the chance of error. It was an exciting summer for a young fellow like myself, camping in the open by a singing creek, listening to the voices of the forest in the evenings, and watching in fascination during the days those dark wrinkled faces and eyes that were both humorous and wise. Sam Brown, the Hoopa interpreter, was a thin gentle man, with a hint of sadness in his face, but with a quick tongue and brain, very helpful in many ways except at the time of the White Deer Skin Dance. Then he arranged for us to pay for permission to take pictures of the dance, without explaining to us what we learned with great suddenness later—that there were two clans involved in the dance, not one.

The two rows of dancers faced each other, both sides with bright orange flicker feather headdresses, and each man holding a beautiful white deerskin, a great heirloom, mounted on a pole he held in front of him. Then, swaying to and fro and chanting one of those strangely moving and beautiful California Indian songs, they bowed the white deerskins back and forth. I was so fascinated I almost forgot to take pictures. At first I was not seen in my photo endeavors until after a roll of film had been used, which I passed over to Mr. Driver after taking it from the camera. I had hardly begun the second roll before a combination of something like thunder and lightning erupted. I heard a deep angry shout and suddenly a group of Indians surrounded me, pushing and shoving and asking how I dared to be taking pictures!

I think my own deep shock and the manifest innocence that shone in my face saved me from further violence. "I have permission! I have permission!" I kept saying over and over.

A dark fierce face was thrust close to mine and a savage voice asked: "Whose permission?"

By this time both Driver and Sam Brown were simultaneously trying to explain who we got permission from, but Sam was shoved contemptuously aside.

"This one should have known better!" said the savage-faced man. "But understand our clan has not been asked permission nor paid, and you can take no more pictures. Give me your film!"

I extracted the film from my camera and handed it to him, while trying to ask if we could not pay now for permission from the second clan. He threw the film on the ground and crushed it savagely with a naked but well-calloused heel. "No!" he shouted, "no more pictures!" And "no-no!" echoed his clan-mates.

Very quietly indeed we watched the rest of the White Deerskin Dance, but I had learned a lesson, which is to never be sure you have permission to take photographs or do anything else with the Native Americans until you are sure that all who take part agree!

Looking back on those fine summer days on the Hoopa Reservation I can see how naive both of us were and how very little we knew about these people. Our copious notes about their material cultures, such as fishing, hunting and plant-gathering methods, their houses and cooking ways, and so on were probably correct enough. Indeed our informants often helped us by taking the actual tools or hunting weapons and baskets and showing us how they were used. But when we talked to them about their social and particularly their religious culture, then a veil we did not understand at the time would fall over their eyes or, at times, a glint of mischief.

Such a glint I am sure peeked out between the deep wrinkles on the face of a 96-year-old Chilula man who told us one day through the interpreter the story of a war between the Chilula and a neighboring village of the Hoopa. One must think of these people as living in deep mountain valleys surrounded by thickly forested ranges and peaks. The Chilula, a very small people, had inhabited for many centuries the thirty-five mile long valley of Redwood Creek, emptying into the Pacific Ocean near Orick, California. Surrounded by more populous peoples, they would have been wiped out long ago had their neighbors been truly organized for war. As in most of California, however, the main political unit was a single large village, sometimes with a few satellite villages around it. Actually in this northwest part of California the people were so individualistic that most of the villagers simply followed the richest man or family, and there were few chiefs in any real sense.

But the old Chilula man told us an elaborate story of a war between the Chilula and the Hoopa, often waxing quite dramatic, while waving his thin wrinkled hands to illustrate it, as we wrote down every word with bated breath! I found out later that many of his people laughed along with him about that great adventure in savage blood-letting, because it had never happened at all the way he told it. We had asked for a war, however, so he gave us one with all the trimmings!

In regard to religions I am sure we were told other similar fictions, or the respondents sullenly backed away from the topic and refused to answer. When dealing with this sensitive subject, I am sure that the sight of our pencils poised over our notebooks antagonized them in much the same way as the ubiquitous tape-recorder used by the more recent anthropologists. Joseph Eppes Brown, the ethnologist who spent eight months with Black Elk, the famous Sioux holy man, recording the deeper meanings of his religion, made certain, I am sure, before he ever started tape recording the words of the old man that he was fully in favor of such a procedure. But other scientists, I know, have been in too much of a hurry to put Indian words on tape and have encountered the same hostility we did with our note-taking. Great tact, courtesy and understanding is necessary between the two races. I have found that I could learn more by coming simply as a friend without either notebook or tape recorder. It is fortunately true that, as in the case of Black Elk, more and more of the old people are realizing that if their stories of the past and particularly of the religion and the spiritual experiences of their people are not put into some kind of permanent form, something of immense value will be lost to their own grandchildren. In truth many a modern Indian today is cautiously feeling his way back to his own past and heritage through the records of ancient culture and religion made by anthropologists. Soon there will be no other way!

It is sad that so many of us, anthropologists, teachers, writers, missionaries and government agents, have come to the Indians with preconceived ideas about them, and often with a blind egotistic idea that we knew better than they did. This attitude has often cost countless wasted days and hours, and much ill feeling among Native Americans who might otherwise have been cooperative.

chapter FOUR

Learning to
Understand and
Reach the Spirit

"In the house of long life there I wander,
In the house of happiness there I wander.
Beauty before me, with it I wander.
Beauty behind me, with it I wander.
Beauty below me, with it I wander.
Beauty above me, with it I wander.
Beauty all around me, with it I wander.
In old age traveling, with it I wander.
On the beautiful trail I am, with it I wander."

Dawn Boy's song on entering White House.

From *Navajo Myths, Prayers and Songs with Texts and Translations,* Univ. of California Publications in American Archaeology and Ethnology, Vol. 5, No. 2, Berkeley, 1907. Republished in *Navajo Wildlands,* Sierra Club-Ballantine Books, 1969.

TO BE SILENT AND TO listen with either the ears of the head or ears of the spirit, and to be in no hurry to start talking is a sign of deep sensitivity and respect for others. It is a hard lesson to learn! Yet only when I remember and learn to be still do I find real spiritual oneness with the Native Americans. Of course many have picked up the white men's ways and have forgotten this power of the silence, but instinctively many come back to the old ways when their souls are touched.

A part of the way back to the spirit of man and the universe is to become like a little child again, listening with that curiosity and intent awareness that children have when they really want to know. It is an opening of the channels of the mind and the spirit—channels too long clogged by our materialism, our emphasis on doing things just to be doing them, going somewhere, seeking pleasure or wanting to be amused without separating out the true reality of life from that which is unreal and ephemeral. The deeper pleasures and knowledge of the spirit can last forever, while the pleasures of the body can be gone in a day or an hour, never to return.

In *The Journey To Ixtlan,* by Carlos Castaneda, the wise Yaqui medicine man, Don Juan, tells Castaneda that the journey to reality has three steps, that of the hunter, the warrior and the man of knowledge. Don Juan's knowledge of this journey goes back through the teachings of his people's many medicine men to the time long ago when the first man of knowledge, probably a culture hero, learned to make the breakthrough into reality and taught the vision of the pathway to his part of the world.

What we need to realize is that many such sacred beings have come to many parts of the earth and brought this knowledge to many different peoples, showing similar though different Pathways of the Dawn. Today, I believe, there is a New Pathway of the Dawn, destined to bring all the earlier pathways together in new dimensions of world understanding and love. But even before we find this new pathway we can learn much from the old pathways if we open our hearts and minds to them, and also learn to be careful of those that lead us astray. Castaneda, for example, was finally taught by Don Juan that the pathways of the drug plants, peyote, thornapple and the sacred mushroom, were really side pathways that could be dangerous, while the best path led through control of body and mind by spiritual power.

My own mistakes have been most numerous and sometimes very painful. Two of the worst mistakes are to become trapped by the desire for pleasure, or to become misdirected, wound-up or paralyzed by anger, fear or anxiety. All are absolute barriers against reaching the spirit, for the spirit of man is a strange thing and a paradox. It cannot become truly free until it is also controlled. And it cannot be truly controlled until it is free of desire, repression, fear and anxiety. And it cannot be free of these until it has learned to relax, but relax dynamically.

What does it mean to relax dynamically? Each person must find his way to do this and your way may be different than mine. I can only make suggestions. To me, to relax dynamically is to let go of everything except the center of the universe which becomes a part of your inner being when your mind, your body—everything about you—becomes still and quiet, allowing energy to flow in and out of you in a circle like a smooth powerful current of water, but all of it coming back to the one point, the center of your body. The mind is aware of a sphere of energy in which the body is centered and is aware of everything surrounding the body without being influenced by it in any way to upset the complete relaxation of body and mind. Into this flow and center comes love, not a love for another being, but an all-encompassing love for all mankind and all life and for the Great Spirit. In this state of dynamically relaxed meditation we prepare ourselves to live life to the fullest as part of a great purpose, to make the world united in harmony and love and to make both spiritual and physical aspects of the earth and its inhabitants beautiful, yet doing so without force of any kind of domination or violence.

To find this control of the mind, body and spirit and this dynamic relaxation is much more difficult for some people than others. For some of us whose emotions, feelings and desires are very strong, it is very hard indeed. This is probably why so many great creative artists, authors, leaders and inventors have lead such tortured lives. Success may literally smash them because it leads them into so many temptations and their strong emotions, not guided by spiritual discipline, fritter away and finally destroy their great potential for creativity and good. I have felt such frittering and known such folly, but the wonderful thing about each of us is that we do have a choice. If we dig deep enough to find the eternal power of the spirit that is within us, we can find the strength to learn from our mistakes and finally overcome them!

You can find many paths to this strength, including the old Indian way of the vision search. There are also other religious routes but a discussion of these would be quite outside the scope of this book.

Some Indians will tell you that a white person can never think or feel as an Indian does, just as some white people say that few or no Indians can ever master the technical know-how of the whites. Both of these statements are based on a natural egotism, not on true knowledge. We like to feel superior to other human beings or feel we have exclusive knowledge they can never have. But the fact is that all of us have exactly the same kind of brain and nerve cells so that our bodies and minds react in the same ways. During pioneer days many white children were captured by Indians and raised in Indian families. Stories are numerous of how Indian they became in feelings, thoughts and actions, so that, when some were later returned, usually by force, to their white families, they were either totally out of tune with them and led most unhappy lives or ran away and back to the Indian life. Also it often happened in the early days of the West or the Frontier that white trappers, particularly Frenchmen, married Indian girls, joined their tribes, and became so Indian in attitude that white men who encountered them later said they acted exactly like Indians!

General Sam Houston lived for awhile with the Cherokees in Georgia when he was a very young man, learning their language and becoming so close to them that he was called by them "The Raven", and often dressed like a Cherokee. Many tribes came to know him as their friend, and once he called them "a race of people whom I am not ashamed to say have called me 'brother'." Thus he could see into their minds and hearts as few white men could and respected the nobility of their character even when they had been so smashed by conquest and broken treaties that a great darkness had fallen upon them.

Some equally remarkable examples have been recorded in history where Indian children were raised in white families and became exactly like them in culture and attitude. An example was described in an article in *The Reader's Digest* some years back, written by a boyhood friend of mine, Reese Wolf. He told how a three-year-old Guarani Indian girl of Paraguay, whose people were totally uncivilized by white standards at the time she was found, was adopted into a French anthropologist's family. She grew up in her adopted white family to become a most cultivated and refined young lady with a college degree and eventually a PhD. in anthropology. At a restaurant in Lima, Peru, where the waiters were Indians and had been brain-washed like many of their race into believing they were inferior to the whites, these Indians were astonished to see a full-blood like themselves acting with such assurance and poise and they could hardly believe that she was real!

In dealing with the Native Americans I have found it possible in some, but not all cases, to break through their barriers of prejudice and distrust towards whites and to begin to build friendship by several vital steps. First is to often observe silence and listen to what they have to say with great respect and interest. Second is to be relaxed with them and completely friendly without getting upset by what they say or do. Many times they have tried to upset me or get under my skin by doing or saying something that indicated their contempt and distrust of the white people and even of me personally. Usually I realize this is a test, and just allow the words to flow over me like water over a duck's back, and take the third step which is to emphasize my great respect for the Indian people and my feeling that they have a great lesson to teach my people about understanding and being in harmony with the natural world. Fourth, if they will listen, I tell them stories from my experiences or from what I have read of the great spiritual and moral power that can be observed in those Native Americans who have in the past or still do maintain a real closeness with the Great Spirit and His creations. These are a people who are following one of the Pathways of the Dawn. Usually these four steps help form a real basis for understanding and friendship.

For example, one day a few years ago when I was on one of several trips to the Hoopa Reservation in northern California, I met an old Indian whom I had met on my first trip there (described in Chapter Three). After some preliminary conversation to renew our acquaintance, I spoke about my interest in the old Indian religion, and almost immediately he tested me. "Oh," he said, "why bother with that, the old Indian religion was just a lot of superstitions!"

"I don't belive that!" I exclaimed. And told him some stories about Chio Jari, the Guaymi Indian boy. When I continued with similar stories about other Indians I had met who showed the power of earth and sky, he shook his head and gave me a strange look. Then, gradually his whole attitude toward me began to change and he finally told me some wonderful stories about a great Yurok medicine man named John Montgomery. John, he told me, received his power by going into the wilderness and praying and fasting several days and nights at a special sacred rock in the mountains until a vision came. He was then able to find lost persons and solve crimes, as well as do other useful feats, by using his psychic powers. This the police on the reservation in time found very useful.

Once two Indian boys left the school in Hoopa Valley at the beginning of a weekend and tried to hike home over the mountains, but became lost for several days. The police searched for them, but could find no sign of them, especially as a rain had washed away all tracks. Somebody suggested calling John Montgomery into the case. John had them take him by car and horseback to the top of one of the mountains between the Hoopa Valley and Redwood Creek. He told them to leave him, but before they were out of sight, they saw him prepare a little fire before which he knelt in prayer. Later one man reported he saw John moving like a dark shadow round and round his fire during the night. In the morning they came back to him, and he pointed towards the great canyon of Redwood Creek, telling them the boys were about fifteen miles away down by the creek. He said: "As you go down the creek, first you will find a place where there are a lot of gopher holes in the damp dirt and there you will find the boys' footsteps. About a quarter mile below that place you will find the boys. One still has some strength, but the other is very weak."

They followed his directions and found the boys exactly where and as he had told them they would! This was only one of several remarkable cases of John Montgomery's powers about which my friend told me.

The question may be asked how I can be sure when such stories told to me are true. The answer is that an awareness of when people are telling the truth or not can be cultivated and grow in power. I believe everybody has some of this sixth sense and it can be developed into a strong thing with practice. Also there are sometimes or even frequently physical signs that show up when a lie is being told, including a particular shine to the eyes and an expression or slight movement of the face that is betraying.

I do not blame the Indians for not wanting to talk to skeptical or scoffing white people about their religion or other intimate things about their culture. Why indeed waste your time on people who will not believe you and also belittle what you believe! Far too many judgments are made of other people and their beliefs without really opening one's mind to investigate and find out the real facts. Native Americans sometimes make the same mistake towards whites, judging them on the basis of their prejudices and not trying to understand them. This is a common human failing of all races.

The purpose of a vision search is not only to find a vision, but also to find in this vision help for yourself to lead a better life and help for other people also. One of the best examples of a vision search that led to a vision that brought help to many thousands of human beings and may eventually bring it to millions comes from Japan. This story emphasizes one important point and that is the oneness of all humanity—meaning that in my view people *of any race* can have great visions of help to themselves and to others. Despite the fact that this story is about a Japanese, the vision search itself and what happened is closely similar to the vision searches of famous Native Americans, and it gives to all of us another worthwhile method to harmonize body, soul and mind with the universe and all men. The vision seeker in this instance made no claim of being a prophet nor of attempting to found a new religion.

Professor Morihei Uyeshiba, who died in 1971 at the age of 87, saw, when he was a young boy, his father attacked by a gang of thugs and beaten badly. At this time he promised himself that he would train and develop great fighting power so he could defend his father and others from such people. Over the years he became an outstanding expert in judo, jujitsu and sword fighting techniques, and also developed a remarkable sixth sense so that he could detect ahead of time the nature of an attack about to be made upon him.

Japan has long been noted for its martial arts, called "Budo—the way of the warrior." But Professor Uyeshiba began to feel in the early 1920s that true Budo meant the protection and harmonizing of mankind, and that it must eventually be developed so it could become "the way of the warrior for peace rather than conflict." Thus he dreamed of developing a new Budo that would be non-violent and yet would be extremely effective in stopping an attack. He also wanted to find something that would be good as long as man lived, since strength would not be vital in its use.

For years he prayed and meditated in the mountains, also studying many religious movements, trying to find ways to reach the Great Spirit and find this new Spirit of the Warrior for Peace that would help all mankind. Sometime in 1925, when he was walking alone in a beautiful garden, the great vision he was waiting for suddenly came over him like a wave of golden light, and he realized how to come into harmony with the universe and with all men, and yet how to defend oneself and others effectively against vicious attackers without doing any real harm to the attackers either.

This new Budo or "Way of the Warrior" is called *Aikido,* in which "ai" means harmony, "ki" means spirit, and "do" means way of, or "the way of spirit harmony". I believe this is very close in its essence to what many great Native Americans also found in vision, and that, as Professor Uyeshiba himself hoped, it is in harmony with the new age of man that is coming in which cooperation and understanding between men will replace conflict and misunderstanding.

Aikido teaches a dynamic relaxation in which one never uses strength against strength, but instead moves as the whirlwind does in the sacred circle. In this state of dynamic relaxation there is neither fear nor anger nor any prejudice. The touch of one's hand on his opponent is light but firm, never resisting, moving with his power whichever way it wants to go, but sucking it into the circle so that suddenly the opponent finds himself flat on his back or face or under the control of a healing but not lasting pain. Through meditation and exercises of body and breath in the silence, the body and mind become harmonized with the spirit and the dynamic sphere of feeling that surrounds you so that, when well-trained, you know exactly when and where and how you are being attacked. Reacting smoothly, swiftly, subconsciously and even lovingly, the attack is either neutralized or turned away so that neither party gets hurt. The warrior has put on a new armor, the armor of the spirit, and this armor, despite its apparent softness, is really stronger and more effective than steel! As Professor Uyeshiba says: "Aikido is not a technique to fight with or defeat the enemy. It is the way to reconcile the world and make human beings one family. The secret of Aikido is to harmonize ourselves with the movement of the universe and bring ourselves into accord with the universe itself. He who has gained the secret of Aikido has the universe in himself and can say, 'I am the universe.'

"When an enemy tries to fight with me, the universe itself, he has to break the harmony of the universe. Hence, at the moment he has the mind to fight with me, he is already defeated. Aikido is non-resistance. As it is non-resistance, it is always victorious. Those who have a warped mind, a mind of discord, have been defeated from the beginning." (The words are those of Morihei Uyeshiba, taken by special permission [Hozansha Publishing Co., Ltd., Tokyo] from the book *Aikido,* by Kisshomaru Uyeshiba, son of the founder, Kowado Publishing Co., 1958.)

I have been studying Aikido and practicing it for the last four years. It is tremendously interesting and of great value in training mind, body and spirit. The wise Indian of the past, he who became a true "Warrior of the Rainbow", knew something of this secret also. He also had found a way to come into harmony with the universe. By training and by vision seeking, he purified heart, body and mind and often obtained great powers to help his people. Thus I think Aikido helps us understand this way of harmony and service in the world today.

Let us now move on to meet some of the great Indian culture heroes who brought a similar spirit and teaching to man in the New World long ago. As will be seen, their teachings were very similar to those of Jesus.

chapter FIVE

Lords of the Dawn

INVOCATION OF DSILYI NEYANI

Reared within the Mountains!
Lord of the Mountains!
Young Man! Chieftain!
I have made your sacrifice.
I have prepared a smoke for you.
My feet restore thou for me.
My legs restore thou for me.
My body restore thou for me.
My voice thou restore for me.
Restore all for me in beauty.
Make beautiful all that is before me.
Make beautiful all that is behind me.
It is done in beauty.
It is done in beauty.
It is done in beauty.
It is done in beauty.

From the Navajo "Night Chant"

The Mountain Chant, a Navajo Ceremony, by Washington Matthews. 5th Annual Report of the American Bureau of Ethnology, 1887, pages 379-467.

THE ABOVE SONG OF THE Navajo subconsciously expresses the meaning of the coming of the culture hero, him who I call here "the Lord of the Dawn." He comes to the people to restore the spirit and make them walk in beauty. Sometimes a culture hero is so far back in the history of a Native American tribe or nation that his teachings and personality become so overlaid with newer legends or ceremonial ways and ideas that he is lost to us or only barely seen. The latter seems to be the case with the Navajo, whose culture hero or heroes are hidden or only briefly hinted at, but whose spirit seems to appear in such songs as the one above. The Navajos do have in legend the story of two sacred twins, called also "the Slayers of Alien Gods", whom legend says destroyed many evil giants, demons and similar beings, but there is no certainty that they also taught any form of religion or moral code. Nevertheless the religion is there and so is the moral code, although it has slipped badly in recent years.

That something much stronger was there in the life of the people at an earlier time was hinted at by an old Navajo medicine man who told me, with a slap of his hand in distaste, that it had recently been almost impossible to find a virgin girl over eleven years of age to hold the pitcher of sacred water at one of the ceremonies. Also he stated that in the long ago they not only had plenty of virgins, but no stealing, drunkenness nor prostitution. Such a story speaks to me of the influence far back of a culture hero, who brought a beautiful message of honor and purity to the tribe. In Chio Jari, the Guaymi Indian youth referred to earlier, I was fortunate to see this kind of purity and honor exemplified in a living human being, and so saw in truth a young man *walking in beauty*.

The beautiful control of such a man over his passions and emotions and desires, a control not to be confused with repression, but a harmony of man with the universe, in the way of the rainbow, the waterfall and the sunrise, in which ugliness of conduct is impossible, is little understood by those who seek what they call "freedom."

The kind of "freedom to do what you want or your thing!", which many people seek today, has always been a sign of decay, and destruction of tribes, nations, cultures and civilizations. It is not true freedom at all, but slavery to self, and this kind of "freedom" is not new. It has happened time and again in history and nation after nation, Greece, Rome, Turkey, Persia, China, and others, have gone down into at least partial decay or destruction because of it. True freedom, as all the great culture heroes and prophets have taught a reluctant mankind through all history, is "freedom from desire and passion", the calm, cool, joyous and beautiful harmony with the universe and with the Great Spirit that builds first strong and united families and then great nations and civilizations, and will build, I believe, in the century to come and in a New Age coming, a glorious and harmonious world.

The culture heroes in America, as elsewhere in the world, usually come to a people troubled by disunity, dishonesty, superstitions, slavery and other customs or taboos that were harmful, occurring side by side with moral collapse, war and hate. These great heroes try, like Moses, to break their people free from idleness and corruption, the worship of many gods or idols, and teach them to see the Great Spirit in everything beautiful, though they may give Him different names than we do and their concept of religion may have qualities and ideas somewhat different from ours. Getting rid of the many gods and the idols seems to be particularly difficult, as is illustrated by the difficulties of Moses with the Israelites during the forty years of wandering in the wilderness of Sinai, and by the similar difficulties of Quetzalcoatl with the Toltecs of Mexico when many of them turned, despite his efforts, back to idol worship and human sacrifice.

People react differently to the culture heroes. Some accept one quickly and become his true servants, which also means servants of the Great Spirit. Others take much longer to accept, and still others may accept him at first and then later throw out the new teachings, as mentioned in the paragraph above. Some people keep the original purity of the teachings going for many centuries, as did the Cheyennes of the Great Plains, while others soon allow themselves to become contaminated with devil worship and other negative aspects of religion in decay.

Some of the more ancient civilizations of the New World, such as the Maya, and the central Mexicans, give evidences of having at least two culture heroes, with a thousand years or more between them. Thus Ce Acatl Tolpiltzin Quetzalcoatl (our Lord, One Reed, Feathered Serpent) of the 10th or 11th century A.D., was considered by the Mexicans not the first Quetzalcoatl, but at least second in a line of such spiritual beings. It is interesting that the high priests of Quetzalcoatl called themselves by this same name also down through the centuries. And the name came to be used for a high god. This repetition of the name for a culture hero is similar to the Lord Guatama Buddha of India foretelling that other Buddhas would come after him, and Jesus speaking of the return of another Christ like "a thief in the night."

Is there not some reason to suspect that this may be all part of a marvelous plan of the Great Spirit woven through the ages and beginning to find fulfillment on a world scale in our time? When we begin to study the prophecies of all religions, we find the same golden thread of a great promise that one day all men will begin to come together in brotherhood, unity and love.

I do not believe it is possible at this stage in our knowledge of Native American culture heroes to make any rigid rules about how they came, or how they can be put into categories. Instead it seems best simply to develop different possible theories about them and then see how further research may prove or disprove these suggested ideas and any others that might be offered. To keep an open mind is to follow the scientific method and gradually come closer and closer to the truth. So the following are some suggested theories or hypotheses:

1. *They were all false prophets who brought only religions that were superstitions and savagery.* This would probably be the idea of some strict religionists who think that every other religion except their own is obviously wrong. But why did Jesus warn us to judge prophets by their fruits? He said if they brought thorns and thistles, meaning teachings that are harmful to people and teach them to stray away from God, then they would be false prophets. But what if they bring or brought "good fruits"? So far as I have been able to find out the culture heroes I shall speak about in this book brought teachings of honor, cooperation, purity and obedience to the Great Spirit, all very close to the moral teachings of Moses and Jesus. They taught the Native Americans prayers, meditations and how to use the vision search not for selfish ends, as some tribes did, but for the good of all the people and to strive diligently to purify heart and mind so they would come into harmony with the Spirit of the Universe. It might be, as was the case with the Sioux, that lesser spirits were spoken of, such as Waziah, the giant of the north, or the Spotted Eagle, and others, but all of these were considered but manifestations of the One Great Spirit, as the Christians and Jews might speak of the spiritual powers of the angels, who, no matter how wonderful they were, were still considered servants of God. I cannot believe these inspiring beings, the culture heroes who brought so much good and honor to the Indian peoples, were false prophets.

2. *The culture heroes were individual manifestations of the Great Spirit, or at least spiritually inspired beings, each sent to different*

peoples in the Americas as their spiritual leaders, but with no connection with each other. This is quite possible, as the legends rarely speak of any connections between the different ones, with the exception of Quetzalcoatl of the Valley of Mexico, and Kukulkan of the Mayas. This would imply, since all taught essentially the same message of purity and goodness, that they either created their ideas as parallel inventions of the human mind, or, what seems more probable, that they were all inspired by the same Great Spirit who gave them each a similar teaching to pass on to the tribes or nations to whom they came.

3. *The culture heroes can be divided into greater and lesser prophets, with the Great Prophet bringing the main message to mankind in America, while the lesser prophets reflect His spirit in different areas.* This would probably make Quetzalcoatl of Mexico, a Great Prophet, whose message was later repeated by lesser prophets in other parts of the Americas. In *Numbers* 12:1-8 in the Bible we find the difference between a greater and lesser prophet explained, when God speaks to Moses, Aaron and Miriam, calling the two last mentioned lesser prophets who received visions, while Moses is described as a Great Prophet to whom "I (God) speak mouth to mouth."

Quetzalcoatl gives the feeling of being a Great Prophet as he speaks with greater authority, his message is more complete than any of the other culture heroes, and it was also much more widely spread. Many of the other culture heroes appear to have come after Quetzalcoatl, which adds some more weight to this theory. Thus we know that Quetzalcoatl appeared probably in the 10th century to the Mexicans, while Degandawidah of the Iroquois, and White Buffalo Calf Maiden of the Sioux occurred probably some centuries later than this from what evidence we have.

4. *The culture heroes can be divided into one or more Great Prophets, and a number of disciples whom they had filled with the Spirit and who carried their message far and wide.* Even a man who came much later than the Great Prophet could be considered a disciple in the same way as the great saints carried the message of Jesus over wide areas. Since Quetzalcoatl is spoken of in legend as sending out four disciples to the four directions to carry his lessons to the Americas, we can think of these disciples developing other disciples who would carry the Message on to still farther areas and even in later times. The greatest surge upward of the culture of the peaceful and cooperative Mound-builder civilization of the Mississippi and Ohio Valleys, for example, began in about the 11th century, and so could have been given spiritual impetus by disciples of Quetzalcoatl at that time. This civilization apparently broke down in the 16th century due to the

spiritual power being lost to selfishness and corruption, as war and rivalry increased. The same thing happened to the Itza-Mayas of Yucatan, followers of Kukulkan (possibly a disciple of Quetzalcoatl), after the League of Mayapan broke up in the 15th century, due probably to the weakening of the religion and increasing friction between ruling groups.

5. *This would be a combination of theories 3 and 4.* We can see that both systems described in the previous two theories, alone or together, can be thought to extend back long before the 10th century A.D. time of the last Quetzalcoatl, to another Quetzalcoatl or Great Prophet of the period 200 B.C. to the beginning of A.D., when both the Mayan and Teotihuacan cultures were just beginning really to flower. Thus the great First Mayan Empire or Confederacy showed a peaceful and cooperative period of about a thousand years between these two times, as did also the wonderful Teotihuacan Culture of central Mexico. About A.D. 800 both of these areas were crumbling into temporary confusion and barbarism, out of which rose around A.D. 1000 the reflowering of Mayan culture in northern Yucatan, and the rise of the civilizations of the Toltecs and Aztecs in the valley of Mexico. It is interesting that the same patterns of culture and cultural conflict appeared at the close of both these periods when warfare, human sacrifice and other evidences of friction and corruption took the place of the times of cooperation and cultural flowering that followed the appearance of a culture hero.

An interesting theory of the Mormons is that Jesus Himself came to America at the time of His crucifixion in the Holy Land and spread His teachings in the New World. Though possible, it seems to me more logical that the Great Spirit would send a messenger to Indians who would be an Indian, but would reflect the same high spiritual qualities and teachings.

It is time now to consider individually some of the culture heroes whose lives we know most about.

chapter SIX

Degandawidah and Hiawatha of the Iroquois

"I am Degandawidah, and with the Five Nations' confederate lords I plant the Tree of the Great Peace . . . I name the tree the Tree of the Great Long Leaves. Under the shade of this Tree of the Great Peace we spread the soft white feather down of the globe thistle as seats for you, Atotahro, and your cousin lords. There shall you sit and watch the council fire of the confederacy of the Five Nations. Roots have spread out from the Tree, and the name of these roots is the Great White Roots of Peace. If any man of any nation shall show a desire to obey the laws of the Great Peace, they shall trace the roots to their source, and they shall be welcomed to take shelter beneath the Tree of the Long Leaves. The smoke of the confederate council fire shall pierce the sky so that all nations may discover the central council fire of the Great Peace. I, Degandawidah, and the confederate lords now uproot the tallest pine tree and into the cavity thereby made we cast all weapons of war. Into the depths of earth, down into the deep under-earth currents of water flowing into unknown regions we cast all weapons of war. We bury them from sight forever and plant again the Tree."

Quoted from the book *I Have Spoken,* by Virginia Irving Armstrong, 1971, Sage Books.

THERE IS NO QUESTION BUT what Degandawidah was the prime mover and the founder of the religion of the Iroquois of the Five (and later six) Nations of the Seneca, Cayuga, Onandoga, Oneida and Mohawks. The Tuscarora joined the League much later. But there is no doubt also that Hiawatha, his chief lieutenant, was such a wonderful and effective disciple that he too should be called a culture hero. This Hiawatha was quite a different person from the one in Longfellow's poem which was probably taken from a legend of the Objibwa.

Handsome Lake, who came much later to the Iroquois and after white conquest, was a visionary believed to be a prophet by those who followed him, but something else to those who did not. He renewed some elements of the religion of Degandawidah, but added some elements of Christianity that antagonized traditionalists among his own people. He did much, however, to save his people from the curse of alcohol.

The brief history of the Iroquois religion that follows is one of several versions, though the outline in general is the same, but the important parts are the spiritual teachings and these are basically the same.

Long before the time of Degandawidah many tribes of the East and Midwest were under the probable influence of a prophet or culture hero whose name is lost to us. It may possibly have been Quetzalcoatl, the Feathered Serpent of ancient Mexico, whose disciples or missionaries could have brought a sky and circle religion to the great central valley of the Mississippi and Ohio. The evidence for some spiritual impact like this is shown in the great and peaceful culture of the Mound-builders that reached a wide expansion in this enormous valley in the 11th century, soon after the life of the Quetzalcoatl. This civilization saw few if any weapons of war, while peaceful trade spread for a thousand miles or more. Beautiful art work was created, many elaborate effigies, and intricate jewelry and pottery. Unlike later times when the warriors refused to do such work, men labored mightily to create vast religious-oriented mounds in the shape of animals and birds where great ceremonies may have taken place.

By the time of Degandawidah, whose arrival on the scene is variously reckoned from the 11th to the 16th century, this peaceful, far-trading, religiously-harmonized culture had probably begun to fade in influence, and in the area of the Iroquois, at least, peace had given way to war, and major trading expeditions had become very difficult if not impossible.

The legend of Degandawidah tells how he was born a Huron, an Iroquois-speaking nation that existed in southern Ontario, Canada, and that he brought a message of peace and high honor to tribes deeply involved in the vicious circle of war and blood revenge. The peace of the Mound-builders had been almost totally forgotten. Every tribe was against every other tribe and no man, woman or child was safe in the eastern and midwestern forests save behind the high-stockaded walls of strongly-fortified villages, a thing unheard of in Mound-builder times. That Degandawidah sought to bring back this peace and almost succeeded speaks of his greatness, and his reflection of the will of the Great Spirit. Whether he and his people would have succeeded in uniting the Indian nations if the white people had not come, no one knows. But it is known that soon after the first white men came they were either destroying Indians or using them as power pawns in the wars between European nations for control of the new continent of America. In so doing they often pushed tribe against tribe, begging and bribing them to fight each other or enemy whites, and in so doing they wiped out all chances to save the peace until the peace of the conquered finally came when white civilization crushed the last Indian resistance.

It is rather strange, but illustrative of true greatness in Indian character that, though the peaceful culture of the Mound-builders disappeared and presumably most of their religion with it, some distinctive parts of this religion remained. Most of the tribes that had been influenced by the Mound-builders, including the Siouian-speaking nations such as the Osage and Omaha, who may have been a direct part of that civilization, and the Iroquoian-speaking peoples, who were probably on the outer fringe of it, continued to worship sky deities, including the sun and moon, and most had a legend of the great Creator God. These people usually recognized the earth as Mother and the sun as Grandfather, so recognizing the duality of the male and female principles in creation, as the Chinese do with their doctrine of the Yin and Yang, the two poles of life. We can theorize that somehow the white people lost the feminine principle of existence by too much emphasis on the masculine and, in so doing, lost the reverence for the earth as a bearer of life and instead looked upon her as a producer to be exploited for profit, and not used with respect and love.

This power of the feminine in Indian religion may also account for the far greater reverence and respect towards women as the bearers of life among Native Americans than we find in European-based culture and religion. Only a very deep feeling of this kind, a feeling that every woman must be protected so she can make the sacred nest of the family in which the children can be reared with honor and goodness, can account for the fact that rape and similar sexual abuse of women was almost unknown among Indian tribes of the East and Midwest at the time of first white contact. There were other tribes and nations in other parts of America that had equally high ideals of this nature, but in other areas it was not quite so widespread.

Degandawidah came not only to renew and reinvigorate these great teachings of past holy people of his race, but to bring a plan of unity and peace. He taught that one must not only give up enmity towards one's enemies, but befriend and help them. The leaders of the new League of Nations he was trying to form must show such strong character that ". . . the thickness of your skin will be seven spans, for you will be proof against anger, offensive action and criticism. With endless patience you shall carry out your duty, and your firmness shall be tempered with compassion for your people. Neither anger nor fear shall find lodgment in your mind, and all your words and actions shall be tempered with calm deliberation. In all your official acts, self-interest shall be cast aside. You shall look and listen to the welfare of the whole people, and have always in view, not only the present but the coming generations—the unborn of the future nation." (From *I Have Spoken,* by Virginia Irving Armstrong, 1971, Sage Books.)

Using a method of secret ballot, the leading chiefs and sachems were elected by the wise women of the League of the Iroquois, generally choosing those whose fine spirit and dignity had been shown in action. These women could also take away the power of a chief who showed foolishness, pride or selfishness in his work. Thus the feminine principle of peace and harmony was given control over the warlike and conflict-producing principle of the male. After a time, nevertheless, and due mainly to the strains of conflict brought on by the struggle of the great European powers to seize parts of America and their subjugation of the Iroquois and other tribes to their aims, the male principle of warfare began to dominate again.

But how did Degandawidah's League of the Iroquois actually start? His own people the Hurons, unfortunately did not listen to his teachings, another classic example of a prophet having no honor in his own country! But when he visited the Onandoga and Mohawk nations of what is now New York State he found some who would listen among these warring people. Among them was an outstanding character-to-be, Hiawatha, who had however until this time lead a life largely of evil and who had succumbed to black despair because his wife and children had been killed by a monster-like human being called Atotahro, who was an Onandogan.

Hiawatha had fled his own people to live for a while among the Mohawks, and here he observed a miracle when the Mohawks asked Degandawidah to climb a tree overhanging a deep gorge, and then cut down the tree! In the crash somehow Degandawidah escaped, convincing many of the Mohawks and Hiawatha that he was a sacred being and that they should listen to his message. Soon Degandawidah so filled Hiawatha with the Spirit that he began to sway the tribes of the Iroquois with his great native powers of oratory, wisdom and courage, something Degandawidah found difficult to do because of a stuttering speech defect.

The two great heroes first persuaded the Mohawks and then the Oneida and Cayuga tribes of the Iroquois to join the new religion and to begin to form a new League of Nations. The Onandoga, however, proved much more difficult, as they were noted for their independent nature, but their suspicions and doubts vanished when Degandawidah and Hiawatha bravely entered the dangerous vale where the slayer of humans, Atotahro, lived. Exerting his eloquence to the utmost, and facing the monster bravely, Hiawatha finally convinced Atotahro that he should change his ways and join the rest of the Iroquois in creating a beautiful league of peoples. Atotahro was also offered a prominent position on the Supreme Council of the League, a position he filled honorably and with distinction the rest of his life.

The Seneca proved even more stubborn than the Onandoga, but the success and happiness of their fellow Iroquois in the League finally convinced them and they joined the League of the Iroquois a year later.

Legend tells us that the mysterious prophet founder of this new religion, Degandawidah, left his people soon after the League was formed and traveled eastward in a sacred stone canoe, never to be seen again. But he left the wise and eloquent Hiawatha in charge and he is the one who deserves credit for much of the fine organization of the Iroquois League. Later Jefferson, Adams, Washington, Franklin and other great leaders of the new United States of America used many of the ideas that had flowered in the League of the Iroquois in their framing of the American Constitution, with its careful limitation of powers and its ideals and plans for government for and by the people. Actually the unwritten constitution of the Iroquois went farther in at least one respect than its descendant, for it taught the sachems or leaders how to find true unity of purpose by giving up the ego. It did this by allowing full freedom of debate among the leaders, but insisted that all selfish thoughts be left behind once a vote was taken on any idea or plan so the League could act with one mind. All later backbiting and argument was strictly forbidden, though a vote at a later time when a course of action proved unworkable always could bring about a change.

It is very sad that the Iroquois League, founded with such hope for peace between nations, perhaps as early as the 11th century A.D., never quite realized the dream of its founder to bring true unity to all the Indian tribes. Though later it became of great military strength and conquered wide areas, the White Roots of Peace were too often forgotten and the Iroquois set out more to dominate than to combine and unify. Increasing the problem were the efforts of the English and the French invaders of America to use the tribes as pawns in their own wars and struggles for the domination of the new continent. The Iroquois were caught up in this dark web of war and intrigue and, despite their great power, eventually destroyed as a force. At last, exhausted and corrupted by all the warfare, they themselves were conquered by the whites.

Degandawidah, like other culture heroes, taught the highest standards of truth, honesty, chastity and kindness, also obedience to government and of children to adults, but these standards began to crumble under the traumatic experience of the conquest and the decline. The sense of defeat and despondency caused many native peoples to turn to alcohol and loose living. The destructive nature of drunken brawls in many Iroquois villages towards the end of the 18th century and the beginning of the 19th became so bad that the Five Nations, now actually numbering six, were in grave danger of going the way of the tribes they themselves had helped to destroy.

It was at this time that one of the worst of the drunkards, a Seneca chief named Handsome Lake, became so sick from his dissipations that he went into an unconscious state for many hours, during which he was given the first of several visions that changed his own life dramatically and helped his people. Handsome Lake now turned away from alcohol completely and began to preach against it, at the same time teaching a return to all that was best in the old Iroquois religion. He also brought elements of Christianity into what he taught, so combining good things of both. In his dreams four spirit beings or messengers, dressed like Indians, but whom he called "angels", appeared to him and gave him guidance, especially in getting rid of the curse of alcohol.

His preaching on this subject was so inspiring that many hundreds of his fellow Iroquois were persuaded to take up the new-old religion of their forefathers in its modern version, as developed by Handsome Lake, and leave their destructive habits behind. Unfortunately, however, he came into conflict with some of the traditional people of the Iroquois, whose secret religious societies he tried to destroy. But he was more successful in his job of trying to end alcoholism, doing much better than the Christian missionaries because he gave his people a sense of destiny and purpose through their own culture and background.

Some missionaries, of course, tried to fight and discredit him although the Quaker missionaries were generally big enough to see that he was doing a lot of good and cheered him on. Later he was criticized for encouraging some of his followers to go on witch hunts and even kill some Indians accused of being witches. Regardless of whether this was true or not, we can see today that Handsome Lake's influence was crucial in preventing the Iroquois from sinking into despair and degeneration. Instead he gave them back pride in their culture and past, built high moral standards, and helped his people again hold their heads high and revived much of the best of their culture.

Degandawidah's, Hiawatha's, and Handsome Lake's dream of the White Roots of Peace spreading peace and understanding between Indian nations seems like a later reflection of a similar peaceful message of Quetzalcoatl given in Middle America some five hundred years earlier. How close they are will be seen in Chapter Nine, but whether there was ever any connection between the two is a mystery which cannot yet be unraveled. Perhaps it can be said that their amazing similarity makes it very likely that they came from the same source.

In the next chapter we encounter a culture hero who was a beautiful woman—both within and without.

chapter SEVEN

The Shining Woman

"With tears running, O Great Spirit, Great Spirit, my Grandfather—with running tears I must say now that the tree has never bloomed. A pitiful old man, you see me here, and I have fallen away and have done nothing. Here, at the center of the world, where you took me when I was young and taught me; here, old, I stand, and the tree is withered, Grandfather, my Grandfather!

"Again and maybe the last time on this earth, I recall the great vision you sent me. It may be that some little root of the sacred tree still lives. Nourish it then, that it may leaf and bloom and fill with singing birds. Here me, not for myself, but for my people; I am old. Hear me that they may once more go back into the sacred hoop and find the good red road, the shielding tree!"

Black Elk, from *Black Elk Speaks,* by John Neihardt;
Univ. of Nebraska Press, 1961.

BLACK ELK, THE FAMOUS HOLY man of the Oglala Sioux, tells us through two books, *Black Elk Speaks* and *The Sacred Pipe,* much of the story of the religion of his people. The above prayer was said by Black Elk when he was a feeble old man and stood for the last time on the top of Harney Peak in the Black Hills, called by the Sioux "the center of the world." The tree he speaks about was the Tree of Life of his people, a spiritual tree, seen in vision, and meaning their closeness to the Great Spirit, or Grandfather. The Sacred Hoop (or circle) was the symbol of the unity in purity and goodness of his people under that tree. During his lifetime he had seen the tree die and the sacred hoop become broken into little pieces under the impact of the coming of the white people, who destroyed the Sioux religion of tribal unity, and replaced it with the divided religion of modern Christianity.

Black Elk was feeling very sad because he had had two great visions, one in 1873 and the other in 1890, of the coming back of the spiritual tree and the Sacred Hoop to his people, meaning their lives would return to the glory and goodness of the best of the old days (see Chapter Fifteen). In his old age nothing like this had happened and his people were still divided and most of their spirit gone so he was beginning to feel that perhaps nothing would ever happen.

But maybe he just did not understand completely his own visions. The coming of great spiritual teachings to mankind in the past has always been through various greatly inspired human beings, such as Abraham, Moses or Jesus, if you are a Jew or Christian; or Krishna or Buddha, if you are a Hindu or a Buddhist, or one of the culture heroes of America, such as Quetazlcoatl or White Buffalo Calf Maiden, if you are of one of the old Native American religions.

It seems reasonable to suppose that if such a great teaching came again, it would be another inspired human being with a teaching for this age of man, since this is the way it has always happened in the past. Too often in the past humans have expected something very spectacular to come and have been fooled when what appears to be just another human being like themselves comes, with the human limitations of pain, disease and death, though with a very beautiful message and life.

But they have looked to His obvious lack of glory and not to His message and been disappointed. This could happen again in the near future or it may have already happened. After all, in the past centuries, after such shining beings have come into the world, distant areas have still not heard about them. Thus it took over four centuries before the words of Jesus reached Ireland from the Holy Land. Thus Black Elk's visions could have come true, at least in the beginning sense, even while he was still alive, for a sacred being could have come, brought a message of purity and unity, and sent this message traveling over the earth with His disciples. None of us can be sure about this one way or another until we search diligently to find out for ourselves.

To the Sioux, about five centuries or so ago, came White Buffalo Calf Maiden (or Woman) with a beautiful message. But it is likely that a similar holy being came in a still earlier time, for the Sioux were given two of their sacred ceremonies long before the coming of the Buffalo Maiden. There is some evidence that Siouian-speaking peoples were the main partakers in the great Mound-builder culture of the Mississippi and Ohio Valleys that lasted for around eight hundred years, until the 15th or early 16th centuries A.D. Since the history of this widespread culture and civilization was one of peace and friendly trade and exchange of ideas, as well as giving signs of great religious ceremonies associated with the giant mounds, it is very possible that this peaceful and spiritual period in North American history was started by a great culture hero and that the coming of White Buffalo Calf Maiden was a return of the same kind of spiritual teachings.

The ancient legend tells us that long ago two young Sioux hunters were out looking for game. They finally climbed a high hill but still saw nothing. Then a small dot was seen far to the north, moving toward the hill. As it came closer it turned into a woman walking gracefully over the prairie carrying a skin bundle. As she came still nearer, they saw that she had on a beautiful white buckskin dress, decorated with dark porcupine quills, and that she herself was very lovely. Then one of the young men desired her and spoke his thoughts, but the other young man warned him: "She is a Sacred Woman; put aside such bad thoughts!"

However, the first young man paid no attention and ran towards her. The girl then smiled and beckoned toward him with her arm, calling: "Come and you shall have what you want!"

But, when he came close to her, a small cloud suddenly descended from the sky and covered the two of them. As the other young hunter approached, the cloud blew away in the wind, and he was shocked to see the girl standing alone, but by her dainty feet lay a skeleton covered with worms!

"He had what he desired, corruption," she said, with a smile. "But be not afraid. Because your heart is pure I will come to help your people. Go to your chief and tell him to order prepared a large teepee, into which I will come and teach you sacred things."

In great awe the young hunter ran back to his people and told the chief, Standing Hollow Horn, as well as others of the miracle he had seen and of the coming of White Buffalo Calf Maiden to teach the people. So they set to work and soon built a huge teepee out of many skins, into which most of the people could enter.

When the girl came they saw her walking across the green grass of the prairie as tall and graceful as the willow and with a tender smile on her face like the smile of flowers. She entered the great teepee in a sacred manner, her feet scarcely seeming to touch the earth, and made a circle around the fire seven times. Then she spoke and her voice was like the song of the little streams laughing over the rocks in the springtime, like the wind whispering among the pines, and like the songs and cries of birds crossing the blue sky, for she was a part of all things beautiful and so a very sacred woman. Her eyes were like two limpid pools mirroring the light of the sun and she looked upon them with such love and kindness and seemed to be looking into them and seeing every good and bad thing, and yet forgiving them and loving them, that many wanted to weep and they loved her as children love a good and kind mother.

"I have made for you seven sacred circles," she said, "and they symbolize the seven sacred ceremonies of the sacred pipe. Two of these you already know, for they were brought to you long ago by a sacred being. These are the Inipi (the purification ceremony), and the Hanblecheyapi (crying for a vision)."

She took from her side the buckskin bundle with its beautiful designs made of porcupine quills and held it before them.

"In this," she said, "is a pipe, which makes this bundle *lela wakan* (very sacred), and you must treat it with such respect that no impure person may gaze upon it. Fill this pipe with sacred tobacco as a sign of your love and the power of the Above One, and through it send your voices in prayer to the seven directions, and particularly to Wakan-Tanka, your Father and Grandfather (Great Spirit)."

Then she took from the bundle the pipe of red stone, while some hid their eyes for they did not feel worthy to see it. With the pipe was a small round stone which she placed on the ground and, as she continued to speak, she raised the pipe with its stem pointing skyward.

"This Sacred Pipe will help you walk on the earth in a sacred manner, for the earth you must consider your Mother and Grandmother and that she too is sacred. The bowl of the pipe is the sign of the center and circle of the earth in which all living things are under the power of Wakan Tanka (the Great Spirit). The buffalo that is carved on the stone represents the four-legged creatures living on Mother Earth. The wooden stem of the pipe represents all the growing plants, who feed and heal us and the animals. These twelve feathers hanging from the base of the stem signify Wambli Galeshka, the Spotted Eagle, and also all the winged peoples of the air. They draw your spirit up into the sky and away from thoughts of foolishness or evil. When you smoke this pipe and pray with it, all these living things and the whole universe are joined to you in a sacred way so you must have respect for and pray for everything that is, and so pray to Wakan Tanka.

"This round red stone that I placed at my feet and which I touch now with the pipe symbolizes the earth, your Mother and Grand-mother. It is your living place and a sign to you also that Wakan Tanka has given you a red day and a red road of goodness that you must follow with a pure and humble heart. Let every dawn be holy to you and a sign of the light that must spread through your soul and drive out all that is dark, for you must remember always to treat every living thing with respect and love, especially all the two-leggeds, for all are sacred to Wakan Tanka. You must work daily with prayers and thoughts to purify your spirit and dedicate yourself in service to your family, your people, all mankind and to the Lord of Being.

"Now I will give you a third Sacred Ceremony, which you shall do when a person dies so that its soul shall be kept on the Sacred Red Road and return to Wakan Tanka, the Father and Grandfather of us all. On that day six people shall be especially blessed, the soul who has departed this life, the man who will use the Sacred Pipe to guide that soul on its journey, and four virgins who will become purified that day and dedicated to lead lives of goodness that shall raise their families and influence all who know them in the sacred ways taught by Wakan Tanka."

She explained all the steps in this intricate ceremony of soul and tribal purification, but she made one thing specially clear when she said:

"It is very important that your girls and young men become purified through the sacred rites of the Sacred Pipe, for they are bearers of the new life and they form the families that must walk in the sacred way in order to surround their children with wisdom, honor, goodness and purity. In the family the husband and wife should become one in thought and deed and one also with the Great Spirit. But if they turn their thoughts from the holy way and think with desire for the bodies of others, then they destroy themselves with self and passion, and deprive their children of the Sacred Water of the Spirit. From such families come the ones who harm the world!''

After telling the Sioux of the third sacred ceremony, she promised them that four more would come to them in vision, making seven altogether, and all would help them on the sacred road, but before she left, she gave a final warning:

"For a long time you will live under the shade of the sacred tree of your love and understanding, and your people will be united in the sacred circle, but the time will come when a dark storm will come out of the east and the tree shall die and the hoop crumble to nothing, though a few will keep the beautiful light alive within their hearts. But in time there will come two new circles, making nine altogether, a new dawn light shall come and a new tree will grow, more glorious than ever before. Remember, at the end of this age, I shall return!''

Here we begin to see the general patterns of all the culture heroes. They come mysteriously, sometimes, but appear as human beings like ourselves and teach a beautiful lesson of harmony, highest honor and purity to mankind, stressing service to others and the Great Spirit. They often promise that after a while a dark time will come when the people become materialistic and forget the Spirit and become divided, but after more years there will be a return of this Spirit. So promised White Buffalo Calf Maiden, Degandawidah, Quetzalcoatl, and others like them; so also warned and promised Jesus. The plot grows thicker. Can you see the answer in the years ahead, or are we yet too blinded by the clouds of darkness and selfishness?

It is interesting that all over the earth the number nine is given in prophecy as a sign of something great and good coming. It is spoken of as nine circles, but also as a nine-pointed star. So the Navajos have a legend of the coming of a nine-pointed star when a new light comes and nine-pointed stars are found carved on rocks by ancient Indians and other peoples in America, Africa and Asia.

A legend startlingly similar to that of the White Buffalo Calf Maiden comes from the Old World. I was fascinated to find in the Legend of King Arthur that Arthur had been raised in the wilderness as a child by the wise seer, Merlin. Merlin taught him the languages of the birds and animals and also the meaning of the Sacred Circle of life. Merlin showed him how to travel in his dreams with one of the winged people, the crow, and also with the four-legged ones of the forest. Thus he was very close to all life, as were the great ones among the Native Americans. Because of the purity of his heart, Arthur was able to pull the sacred sword of kingship out of the great stone, and thus became King of Britain. Knowing the Sacred Circle from Merlin, he created the famous Round Table around which the famous knights of the kingdom gathered each year at Pentecost. Here they took the sacred yearly oath to lead lives of goodness and of honor, helping the poor people, protecting all children and women, being of service to all, and being each completely faithful when they married. From the Round Table and the honor of King Arthur and his knights rose a great Christian kingdom that held back for a time the pagan hordes and protected all the people of the land with equal justice. No wonder the people came to King Arthur and blessed him and told him their doors and gates were open because there were no thieves anymore!

In time Merlin left Arthur comforted and strengthened for his great task, while Merlin went away with a Sacred Woman into the mountains of Wales to a secret cave where she caused him to lie down on a stone slab. Here she told him to go to sleep and that he would sleep through the centuries until the Logres (the Sacred Circle) came back. But as the sign of the bigness and greatness that was coming, she wove around him where he slept *nine sacred circles*.

Are not these then the same as the nine sacred circles promised the Sioux by White Buffalo Calf Maiden? Perhaps in these marvelous legends and signs the secret ways of the Great Spirit are being revealed to us. Would it not be wise to open our hearts and minds and seek diligently for the answers?

chapter EIGHT

He Who Brought the Sacred Arrows

"Our father has come,
Our father has come,
The earth has come,
The earth has come;
It is rising—Eye-ye!
It is rising—Eye-ye!
It is humming—Ahe-e-ye!
It is humming—Ahe-e-ye!"

Song composed by Porcupine, northern Cheyenne Ghost Dance leader, from the book *The Ghost Dance Religion,* by James W. Mooney. 14th Annual Report of the Bureau of Ethnology, Smithsonian Institution, 1892-1893.

THE SONG GIVEN ABOVE SINGS of the coming with a humming noise of a new world of harmony and beauty to replace this old world of ugliness and conflict. The Cheyennes, along with many other tribes who followed the Ghost Dance religion in 1890-91, expected their dance to bring back the good days of old. They were disappointed and saddened when this beautiful world did not come right away. But to make a beautiful, harmonious and just world for all peoples will take a great deal of work by more and more millions of people.

The Cheyennes were a great and heroic people and they can regain these qualities again, although many of them seem to have gone into a long sleep, just as Sweet Medicine, their famous culture hero prophesied before he died. They are a people who had one of the greatest groups of heroes and heroines of all time, the men and women under Dull Knife and Little Wolf, who in 1878-79 led their band north from the Southern Cheyenne Agency in Oklahoma in an attempt to return to their natural home in Montana. Several white armies closed in on this ill-clothed, ill-armed and poorly-fed band, as winter also approached, but again and again they escaped until at last starvation, weakness and cold forced them to give up just short of their goal. But there, in northern Nebraska at Fort Robinson, they were imprisoned like dogs in a kennel-like building, where, on the night of January 9, 1879, amidst snow and below zero weather, they made their last heroic attempt to escape. Again they almost made it home, but were finally trapped in a canyon by warmly-clad soldiers and most of them killed. Few sadder stories exist of savage brutality and lack of understanding towards a very wonderful people.

Yet even in the sadness of their long sleep there is something about the Cheyenne people that makes me feel very close to them in spirit. They are still a warm and impulsive people, open-faced and open-hearted. My first meeting with them was in the summer of 1965 when I took my family and the twelve-year-old son of some friends on a trip to visit many tribes. At Lame Deer, Montana, on the Northern Cheyenne Reservation, I saw a group of Cheyenne men seated under the shade of some trees talking, two of them being young men, the other four much older. When I waved to them they waved back and, on impulse, I took over to them a gift copy of a book on which I had collaborated with an Eskimo (William Willoya) called *Warriors of the Rainbow—Strange and Prophetic Dreams of the Indian Peoples.*

Of the group, three whose names I remember were Charley White Dirt, an older man who spoke little English; Francis Black Horse, a young man, and John Stands-in-Timber. The latter, who was tall and straight like his name, had a face I shall always remember for its strong and honest look, but the rest were all fine-looking men, too. John was in his eighties at the time, but seemed quite healthy and could speak good English. He is dead now, but the author of a fine book on his people, called *Cheyenne Memories,* the result of his being the historian of his tribe.

It was John Stands-in-Timber who thumbed through my book as I sat silently with the group, stopping here and there to translate some of it into Cheyenne. After a bit Charley White Dirt spoke to him in

Cheyenne, and John translated, saying, to my pleased surprise: "We all feel this book has a good and strong spirit. We are happy you have given it to us."

We camped that night on the reservation, but the next morning I went looking for the group again and found John Stands-in-Timber and Charley White Dirt standing near the same place as before, but with two new men. John said to me: "Charley wants to say something to you very important."

Charley White Dirt let loose at me a string of Cheyenne that I could not understand except that I realized he was speaking with the utmost earnestness. Then John translated for him:

"He says that soon he and three or four others of our people are going to Bear Butte, our Sacred Mountain, the place where Sweet Medicine had his great vision. They are going to seek visions and they want you to go with them and also help pray for the peace of the world!"

I was thrilled to the depths of my being by these words, as I realized these men had accepted me in their spiritual adventure because of the words written in *Warriors of the Rainbow,* but immediately I was overwhelmed by the greatest sadness, for I realized I had other commitments that I could not get out of.

When regretfully I declined, but saying I would hope to try again another year, I then asked John Stands-in-Timber who Sweet Medicine was.

"He is the Sacred One who brought us our religion," he said, "and told us what would happen to us. He is the Great One who came to our people long ago."

From John then, and from other sources later, I learned the strange and wonderful story of Sweet Medicine, which I give here in shortened form.

Some say Sweet Medicine was born of a virgin, and this is often claimed for other culture heroes, but it may possibly have been picked up later by Indians from the missionaries, because of their claim for Jesus of virgin birth. Regardless of how they were born, all the culture heroes showed many signs of spiritual power and greatness and taught beautiful messages of unity and high moral standards to their people.

It is claimed that Sweet Medicine's mother abandoned him because she was ashamed there was no father, but he was found and adopted by an old couple who called him their grandson and then gave him the name, Sweet Medicine. Others say he was raised by his own father and mother. In any case, even as a young boy he showed great spiritual power and knowledge and did several miracles. One was to put an old buffalo calf skin into a hoop, then strike it through the center with a magic arrow that changed it into a living buffalo calf.

As Sweet Medicine grew older he began to learn to hunt, but the very first buffalo he hunted got him into trouble with his tribe. He was alone when he shot and killed a yellow calf (some say a black two-year old), but as he was skinning it, an old man came up and found him with it. Some say it was a chief who found him with this hide. The old man told him he wanted the hide, and this does sound like a chief as in those days, powerful men often used their power for selfish ends. But Sweet Medicine went right on skinning and told him he would give the old man half of the meat, but that he, Sweet Medicine, needed the hide. This made the man angry. He came over to seize the hide for himself, threatening to "whip you if you do not let go!" while swinging Sweet Medicine around and trying to jerk the hide away from him. At this Sweet Medicine angrily lifted up an old buffalo bone that was lying nearby and struck the old man, knocking him out!

When news of this reached the village, brought by other hunters, the people began to boil with anger, especially those of the soldier societies. As to the latter, it must be understood that in this era before the teachings of Sweet Medicine were brought to the tribe, the people were controlled by soldier societies that often used their power for selfish and evil ends. Many people were terrorized by them. Sweet Medicine nevertheless returned home with his bundled hide and some meat from his kill, but he warned his grandmother (or mother) to be prepared to tip the soup pot into the fire the minute any men started to come into the teepee to get him.

Soon the soldiers arrived, and when the grandmother answered their shouts with "yes, he is here!" she tipped the soup pot into the fire, making a loud explosion, a hissing of steam and a cloud of smoke and ashes that rose up through the smoke hole of the hut. When the men rushed inside they found Sweet Medicine gone!

This started many months of hide-and-seek, during which people sighted Sweet Medicine in different localities, the soldiers always trying to surround and capture him, but he always seemed to escape in the nick-of-time, some people saying he turned into a coyote or bird and ran or flew away just when about to be captured. He wore different costumes each time, but the fifth time he was seen in a buffalo robe, holding a peace pipe and with an eagle feather struck through one braid of his hair. This was the costume and insignia worn at that time by a Cheyenne chief.

Finally he disappeared and did not come back until four years had passed. While he was gone the tribe had a very hard time finding food and came near starvation. When Sweet Medicine returned, he found a group of boys hunting food and magically produced a quantity of buffalo meat for them. The tribe heard about this miracle and forgave him his supposed misdeed. At his command, they also prepared a special teepee for him, as he told them he was coming with great power to help his people.

The stories about Sweet Medicine diverge at this point, differing widely on what he did next. One version has him come into the teepee and tell about his trip to the Sacred Mountain, Bear Butte (in western South Dakota), where he went into a cave and met the Sacred People, representatives of the Great Spirit, who gave him a spiritual message for his people. In the other version he comes to the teepee where the great chief gives Sweet Medicine his daughter in marriage. Sweet Medicine thereupon lives with the people for four years, helping them to get plenty of food. It is after this, then, that he goes, taking his wife with him to the Sacred Mountain where he meets the representatives of the Above One in the cave and learns from them the message he is told to take to the people.

It is unimportant which of these stories is right. What is important is the message he brought to the Cheyennes. When he comes with the message this is how the story goes: As he comes towards the teepee, he calls to all the people:

"Plains People! Present and future children of the Plains People! With me I bring four Sacred Arrows, wonderful and holy. They will make you strong and good, changing your lives to helping each other, making you a great people! They come to us from the Above One."

When he entered the teepee they were amazed at how fine-looking he was, his eyes looking at them with such love and friendship, all his movements gracefully expressing his unity with them, while he held himself with the expressive dignity of a truly great chief. Essentially this is what he said:

"To be a great people is not just to be fine hunters and famous warriors. The Great Spirit thinks it is far more important for us to be good and kind to one another, so that we don't look down on other people, but help them with love and understanding, for all, even the least, are children of the One Creator. You have been fighting among yourselves and fighting with other tribes without any meaning except selfishness. Now you must think of all people and try to find harmony with them, smoking the pipe of peace even with those who have been your enemies.

"Every day you must turn to the Spirit to get spirit-power, praying not only in the dawn when the growing light tells us how we should be in our hearts, but at noon, at the sunset time and just before you go to sleep, praying sincerely from your heart and not just with your mouth. If you see there is a job to be done, help the people start to do it, and the rest of you when you see that man or woman starting such work, help him or her. If you see there are children without mothers or fathers, take them into your family and make them part of it with all your love. But teach them and your own children also obedience to the laws of life I give you, and be always firm with them as well as good, for children must learn to obey and respect their parents. If you see there are old and infirm people or those who are weak for other reasons, as are widows, bring them the best food and take care of them. But you who are cripples or otherwise infirm, never give up trying to do something to be of help, even if it is only stirring a pot, for out of helping others comes life's purpose and meaning.

"Turn away from lies as you would from fire. Lies lead to death in the spirit. A man or woman of honor would no more tell a lie than chop off their hands with a hatchet. Be trustworthy always and do what you say you are going to do even if it causes you pain or difficulty. But also be humble as the earth, our Mother, for she gives us everything we need and yet allows us to walk upon her.

"Remember there is a special magic and holiness about the girl and the woman. They are the bringers of life to the people, and the chief teachers of the little children. How can they lead the pure-hearted little ones unless they themselves are pure? Protect the purity of their virtue and train each girl to avoid all closeness with men until she is married. Then, when the marriage is made, if done with carefulness, love and knowledge of each others' characters, it will be in the Sacred Circle in which harmony and love and strength surround the children so they grow great in the spirit like their parents. Train the young men to look on girls and women as sacred beings, to be protected from harm, so that their thoughts about them are filled with the same worship and purity as when they look at a beautiful rainbow or a marvelous waterfall splashing down from the cliffs. Then will they make of marriage a treasure of beauty, and their children shall be as arrows of light that spring from them into the future.

"Now if one among you becomes evil, and this happens most often when a family is broken by quarrels and there is no honor between husband and wife, then try with all your might to bring this evil one back into the light. If he asks for forgiveness, forgive him, even many times, as long as he shows remorse and tries hard to be good. But make him pay by working for others or giving of what he possesses to help make up for the harm he has done. If he continues to be a danger to the people, warn him twice that he will soon be sent away as an outcast from the tribe with every man's hand against him. If he does not heed either warning, then come to him a third time and drive him forth forever from the people, warning that if he ever comes back he will be killed, for this is the law to protect the nation from poison!''

Sweet Medicine also set up special ceremonies to reinforce his teachings, and ways for the children to be trained for life and marriage so that they would be in harmony with others. He developed four special honor societies with high moral standards to protect the people both inside and outside the camps. Also he developed a method of electing chiefs and seeing that they properly carried out their duties so the unity and character of the nation could be upheld.

The four Sacred Arrows were renewed in the Spirit at special Grand Ceremonies whenever the tribe showed a weakening of the Spirit. Two of the arrows had special power in hunting, and the other two in war, when war was needed to protect the nation. The arrows were kept always in a special teepee, inside a sacred skin bag and were displayed only at the ceremonies by the Sacred Arrow Keeper. Unfortunately, much later these arrows were stolen by another tribe, and not returned until comparatively recently. While absent, the fortunes of the Cheyennes went down and down!

The new soldier societies, the Swift Foxes, Elks, Red Shields and Bowstrings, were very different from the old soldier societies that had been used to intimidate and exploit the people. After Sweet Medicine these societies were looked up to with respect and love, for their duty was to protect all with equal justice.

Sweet Medicine, it is said, lived for so many years that several generations passed while he was still alive, but finally the time came for his death. It is believed to have happened in what is now Wyoming near the great rocky pinnacle called the Devil's Tower, but some say it happened west of Bear Butte. At the time of his death he gave his last prophecy and warning. He told of the coming of horses, which would be good for the people by furnishing them with swift rides, but told also of the coming of white strangers, who would kill off most of the animals and birds, and who would push in more and more upon the Cheyennes, until they began to take away their blood, by which he meant their children. He said this would make them lose the sacred ways so they would become a lost people. He was very sad about this, and kept repeating: ''Don't let them take our blood!''

Sweet Medicine is one of the few culture heroes of whom we have no record of his promising that eventually the Spirit would return to the people with the coming of another Sacred Being, but perhaps he did say this and somehow it was forgotten.

chapter NINE

The Great Feathered Serpent and the Brotherhood of the Tree

THE LORD OF THE DAWN

"The Lord of the Dawn is coming,
Coming with precious feathers
He is coming,
Carrying a serpent staff
He is coming.
The Giver of Life is coming
The Lord of the Dawn is coming.

From *Lord of the Dawn*—Quetzalcoatl, by Tony Shearer.
Page 65, Naturegraph Publishers, 1971.

CE ACATL TOLPILTZIN QUETZALCOATL, which means in the Nahuatl language, "Our Lord, One Reed, Feathered Serpent," was certainly the most spectacular of all the culture heroes of America and the most widespread in his influence. Very possibly we can put on him the label of being "the Great Prophet of the Americas." There are strong possibilities that he traveled at least as far as Yucatan, the land of the Maya, and to Oaxaca, the land of the Zapotecs, as well as in his more familiar territory of the Great Valley of Mexico. There is even a whisper that he wandered south to Central and even South America, where he could have become known variously in Panama as Ngobo Ulikron, in Columbia as Nemterequetiba, and in Peru as Viracocha (see Chapter Ten). There are still stronger possibilities that he sent out disciples and saints to other parts of the Americas to carry his message of goodness, honor and peace.

There are some hints in the great legends that the Quetzalcoatl motif goes way back to an earlier hero or prophet who taught a new religion in Middle America before or about the time of Jesus and helped spiritually invigorate the cultures of the first Maya Civilization, also that of the great and famous city of Teotihuacan in south central Mexico. At Teotihuacan there are very ancient wall carvings of a man carrying the quetzal feathers and the snake that symbolize Quetzalcoatl. In other words, the "feathered serpent" meant in ancient Mexico the coming of a "Lord of the Dawn", a human being filled with the Spirit of the Eternal, who came in a different body, different character and different soul at different times in ancient American history, but brought the same message of love and honor, cooperation, honesty and kindness that all Christ-like beings bring.

In the *Book of Mormon* there is a reference to the coming of Jesus Christ to America. Non-Mormons, however, might conjecture it as more likely that an Indian prophet of spiritual power similar to that of Christ came at that time to the people of Middle America; it might have been one such as Quetzalcoatl. Still, even if He was the same kind of sacred being, what difference would it make?

There is so much legend and myth surrounding the story of Quetzalcoatl that it is very hard to know when we have the real truth. But legends containing no provable facts nevertheless may have within them spiritual meanings and truths to be watched for carefully. What we do know is that a human being came to the Valley of Mexico around the 10th or 11th century A.D. who had the name Ce Acatl Tolpiltzin Quetzalcoatl, who overcame great difficulties to become king of the Toltecs, who built a most marvelously beautiful city of flowers called Tollan (or Tula), that he established a rule of peace, order and justice, teaching a religion of high honor, love and responsibility, that he was driven from Tollan by his enemies, but continued to spread and teach his religion in other parts of Mexico.

The important thing about his life was the new religion he brought, which will be examined later. Right now it is important mainly to show the background for his advent and then try to weave some life onto the bare bones of the facts so that we may grasp some of his personality and spirit. The legends give much evidence of the existence in those days of a very wonderful human being, but which parts of these legends are facts may be forever unknown.

The historical background of the coming of Quetzalcoatl, the Lord of the Dawn.

Quetzalcoatl is supposed to have lived for about half a century somewhere between A.D. 940 and 1070, with one date span given of A.D. 943 (the year "One Reed" by the Mexican calendar) to A.D. 999. However, other writers give other dates.

The situation in Mexico and northern Central America, the seats of the Maya Civilization to the south and the remarkable Teotihuacan (City of the Gods) Civilization to the north, was very chaotic in the century and a half preceding A.D. 943. Teotihuacan had fallen to barbarian invaders from the north sometime near A.D. 750, but the city of Cholula, its twin to the south in the Valley of Mexico, carried on Teotihuacan culture for at least a half century more (see map number 1, in which Cholula is called Chollolan). The new invaders, probably the first Chichimecs (Nahuatl-speaking) from the north, did not become civilized for a century or so and during this time they spread war and upset through much of the north, but they did not reach the Maya in the south until later. The Maya, however, were having plenty of troubles of their own making, and what has been called "the Great Maya Collapse" of the cities in Guatemala and southern Yucatan, occurred around A.D. 800 to 850. Over wide areas these cities were abandoned and the population decimated to a fraction of their former numbers.

Recent studies by eminent archaeologists have supposed this collapse to be due to a combination of factors, of which the three most important seem to be: (1) political weakening of the ruling class due to intercity rivalries and wars, over-exploitation of the lower classes and an out-of-balance economy in which there were too few workers and too many princes, priests and nobles; (2) the breakdown of trade in food and other vital commodities due to inter-city rivalry and war; and (3) agricultural failure due to pests, overworking the soil, water failure, war, and the growing collapse of leader control.

It is astonishing how few scientists attach much importance to the possible breakdown of religion as a contributing factor to this downfall of civilizations. The neglect of this factor may be due to the materialism of our times in which, to some people, religion seems too mythic or imaginative for acceptance by the pragmatic mind. Actually the rise and fall of many other civilizations in the past, such as Greece, Rome, Persia, etc., have been admitted by many historians as largely due to a rising religious impetus in the beginning followed by a decline as religious teachings became rigid and men went through the motions of worship without awareness of their real spiritual values.

Religion, when faithfully followed and filled with the spirit of love, reverence and creativity, produces cooperative people who work together to create a comparatively harmonious civilization, as apparently was achieved by the early Mayans and the people of Teotihuacan for nearly a thousand years. Of course other factors helped cause a cultural collapse, as already noted, but they are mainly subordinate to the main theme, which is temporary loss of the human spirit through the rise of selfishness.

In the time of great confusion between A.D. 800 and 950 in Middle America, different peoples were contending for power, and other peoples were fleeing to new homes before the advance of conquest and from fear (see Map No. 1). Out of all this confusion would eventually rise the famous Toltec Empire and the beautiful city of Tollan, whose crowning gem was to be Ce Acatl Tolpiltzin Quezalcoatl, ruler and prophet.

Map No. 1 shows the situation at the beginning of this period when the barbarian hordes of the Toltec-Chichimec, yet to be civilized, were coming down out of the north with another savage fighting people, the Otomi. Cholula, or Chollollan, was desperately trying to hold fast to the remnants of Teotihuacan culture, while many of the Teotihuacan nobles, artisans, artists and wise men, now called the Pipiles, were fleeing southward, some even as far as Costa Rica and Panama, trying to find places of refuge.

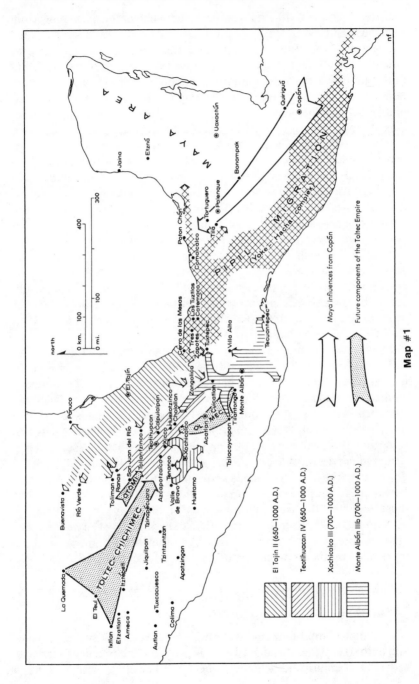

Map #1

Just a bit to the south and west of the advance of the barbarians from both north and southeast, a beautiful mountain valley fortress city called Xochicalco, braced itself for the impact of the Toltec-Chichimecs by building its walls higher and strengthening allied armies to the north and east. This city had a history going back to before 200 B.C. and a long line of priests of the first Quetzalcoatl, through which, the beauty and purity of this earlier religion had been much better preserved than in any other area. In fact, the legends tell us that Xochicalco had priests who knew the exact date when the new Quetzalcoatl—the Lord of the Dawn —would make his appearance and lead those who listened to him to glory. So do prophecies go back and back to the dawn of time!

Other people playing a part in this great living drama of a climactic and changing age were those of the El Tajin culture, a culture developed by a mysterious people of great artistic ability on Mexico's Gulf Coast. Out of the south were coming an equally mysterious people, the historic Olmec, or Tenocelome ("out of the tiger's mouth"), as John Paddock calls them, who were probably a mixture of semi-barbaric Mixtec, Nahua and Cheho-Popoleca peoples. They were called "historic Olmecs" because some elements of their culture resembled those of the far more ancient civilized people, the Olmecs of La Venta on the Gulf Coast near modern Vera Cruz.

These newer Olmecs were soon to conquer Cholula about A.D. 800 and establish a tyranny that lasted about 500 years. Their coming vastly increased the flight to the south of the remnants of the great Teotihuacan civilization, called the Pipiles. (Map No. 1.) These people included the wonderful artisans and builders, the Nonoalca, the philosophers and other wise men called the *Tlamatinimes,* and the renowned artists and sculptors, the Amanteca. Another people moving out of the south at this time, but not destined to come as far as the Olmec-Mixtecs did, were the Zapotecs of the famous civilized and highly artistic city of Monte Alban. It was these people, more than any others north of the Mayans, who most reflected the tremendous genius of the Maya in the fields of astronomy, mathematics and historical dating. They even built special observatories for studying the stars. And they also, in turn, would be influenced by the new religion of the second Quetzalcoatl.

The great adventure of Quetzalcoatl

Mixcoatl (Cloud-Serpent) was the famous Toltec-Chichimec ruler and hero, (see Maps 2 and 3), who was probably the premier founder of the Toltec Empire and believed to be the father of Ce Acatl Tolpiltzin

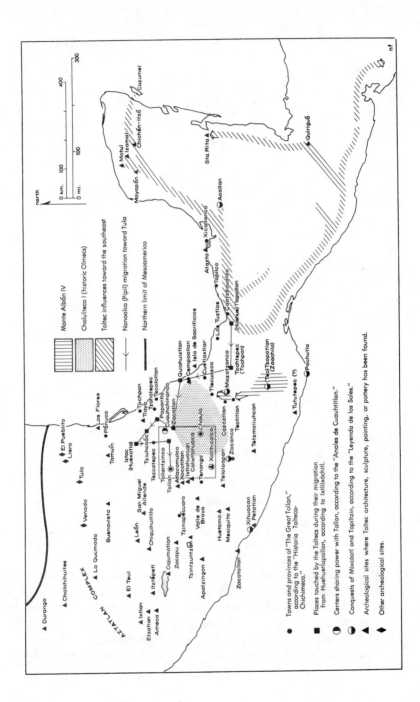

Towns and provinces of "The Great Tollan," according to the "Historia Tolteca-Chichimeca."

Places touched by the Toltecs during their migration from Huehuetlapallan, according to the "Anales de Cuauhtitlan."

Centers sharing power with Tollan, according to the "Anales de Cuauhtitlan."

Conquests of Mixcóatl and Topiltzin, according to the "Leyenda de los Soles."

Archeological sites where Toltec architecture, sculpture, painting, or pottery has been found.

Other archeological sites.

Monte Albán IV

Cholulteca I (historic Olmecs)

Toltec influences toward the southeast

Nonoalca (Pipil) migration toward Tula

Northern limit of Mesoamerica

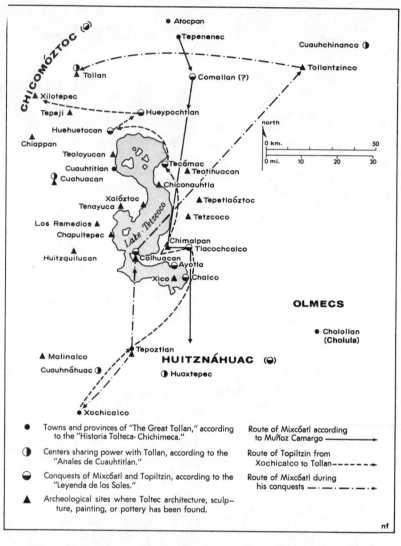

Map #3

Quetzalcoatl, though some legends have Quetzalcoatl born of a virgin. Mixcoatl must have been quite a person, because later he was worshiped as a god. It is told in some legends that Chimalma, a virgin of the Temple of the Dawn at Xochicalco, and so dedicated to the ancient first Quetzalcoatl, was the mother of the new Quetzalcoatl.

When journeying alone one time or another with a small retinue,

Mixcoatl was said to have seen Chimalma near the home of her father and mother at Tepoztlan, while she was bathing in a pool beneath a beautiful waterfall. He fell in love with her. Stories tell how she was as lovely as a dawn goddess with long black hair sweeping down her back as lustrous as silk, that she walked as the willow sways in a gentle wind, and danced more gracefully than the fawn in springtime. Lovely also was she in spirit for it is said children came to her as moths flock to a bright light, and laughed with delight at the sound of her lilting voice, or listened with mouths open to her marvelous stories of the great days of their people and the heroes of the past.

Mixcoatl was a man of great power and strength and of noble bearing, though he was much older than Chimalma. As a noted warrior and leader of chanting armies of the Chichimec-Toltec barbarians, he had conquered many provinces of the once famous Teotihuacan Empire (see Maps No. 2 and 3). He could have captured and carried away Chimalma as easy as a swallow plucks an insect from the air, but he chose instead to court her honorably. Indeed, his heart was so mellowed and tamed by this beautiful girl that he swore he would bring justice and kindness to all his realm, ending the lust and destruction of war.

The marriage was scarcely consummated before Mixcoatl was involved in a titanic struggle with his jealous brothers who desired the control of the new Chichimec-Toltec Empire with all its wealth and power. By treachery they won and Mixcoatl was killed, bringing suddenly into extreme danger the life of Chimalma and her unborn baby. Chimalma fled as the fleet deer flees before the clamor of the hunters.

Chimalma's baby was born on the day *One Reed* (Ce Actl), which can only happen once every fifty-two years, and even then the child had to be born early in the dawn on the first day of the Spring Equinox and at the same moment when the Morning Star (Venus) showed itself on the eastern horizon to fulfill the prophecy and be truly the birth of the Lord of the Dawn. The new baby fulfilled all these requirements and then went on to survive the supreme test of winning his birthright on his twentieth birthday, as detailed on the following pages. Thus he won the sacred name of Quetzalcoatl by being born on the right day of the right year and on the right hour, so obtaining the secret knowledge of Earth and Sky and becoming Lord of the Dawn.

Some say the baby was born in a hiding place near Tepoztlan, but a more likely story is that Chimalma came exhausted and wilderness-scratched to the great Quetzalcoatl-worshipping city of Xochicalco where she was made safe from the barbaric conquerors of the north behind its vast fortified walls. Here she lived with her Uncle Salavi, a Priest of Quetzalcoatl and one of the forerunners and foretellers of the

Lord of the Dawn, whose name became famous enough to reach even as far north as the Hopi, in what is now Arizona. However, when Chimalma's baby was born, her beautiful spirit passed away, it is said, to meet her great warrior husband, Mixcoatl, in a paradise behind the Morning Star.

There are so many stories of the intriguing and powerfully spiritual life and influence of Ce Acatl Tolpiltzin Quetzalcoatl that one cannot help but believe his was a magic childhood. No doubt he was raised by the virgins of the temple and spoiled as a bright happy little boy would be for a while, by doting women. Probably he listened wide-eyed to stories about his lovely mother, drinking in to his being her blythesome spirit, but to tales of his father, Mixcoatl, the great warrior-king, he must have listened with awe and wonder.

When he was old enough, perhaps at the age of seven or eight, I am sure he was taken in hand by one or more of the *tlamatinime,* the wise men or priests of the Temple of Quetzalcoatl and taught to become a man. Probably his great Uncle Salavi, who passed away about this time, selected before his death a worthy man to teach the boy, for one day he was to be filled with wisdom and noted for his courage, one destined to rule nations and change hearts towards the spirit.

Ce Acatl, as he was probably called as a child, must have been a boy of immense curiosity and sensitivity, one who learned to run in the woods and meadows, feeling every touch of the grass on his feet as the touch of living sentient beings, putting his hands on the deeply-grooved and gnarled bark of the ancient oak trees and feeling their immense strength and marvelous growth. They too must have felt his understanding and love, and perhaps even the wind talked to him through rustling tree leaves, until trees, wind and boy became one and he knew—as the truly gifted know—the music behind all living things. The old *tlamatinime,* a woodsman also, taught him to sit still for hours and listen to the birds and animals, until shy forest deer, tree squirrels and monkeys, rabbit-like pacas and other cautious forest folk, came to him like lost children come to an older brother, to take food from his hands. The winged people heard his whistle, and warblers and thrushes sang back to him, while many feathered beings came to perch upon his fingertips and cock their little heads at him in fearless love. He might even have met the Little People, (the Taloque Spirits) the quick sprites of leaf and hollow, the Guardians of the Earth Mother, who the old people say once haunted every sacred wood until the white people came with their loud talk, their killing and their doubts and skepticism, to drive these little folk to the farthest wildernesses.

The *tlamatinime,* I am sure, marveled at the boy and his quick grasping of the meanings of all things as the wisest men knew of them in those days, plus his boyish wisdom and insight, like that of the twelve-year-old Jesus in the Temple of Jerusalem, that was far beyond that of the wisest of men. How could it have been otherwise, for this boy was to be far from an ordinary man in his ability to delve into the worlds of the spirit and the mind? So the old one sat with young Ce Acatl under the stars, stars far brighter then than those tarnished today by haze and smog, and pointed out the bright lights of the constellations and named for him the planets until the boy made playmates of the celestial spheres, calling them by name and following their passage through endless space.

By day he studied the startling Mexican mathematics with its wonderful concept of the zero that the ancient Maya had discovered hundreds of years before it was understood in the Old World. And he learned of the histories of the great peoples of Mexico and Central America, that some of the *tlamatinime* had preserved in beautifully illustrated full-color and hand-drawn books of pictographs, great books later to be so foolishly and viciously destroyed by the narrowly religious Spanish priests. So he learned of the Maya and their mysterious cities of Copan, Palenque, Tikal and many others; also the great City of the Gods, the temple and pyramid-studded Teotihuacan, that had disseminated learning and culture, peace and trade for a thousand years throughout Central Mexico.

So also he learned of the new warlike people coming down out of the north, the barbaric Chichimec-Toltecs, of whom his father had been king, but in his mind grew no glorification of the arts of war. The *tlamatinime* showed him how slowly these people would become civilized as they learned more about Teotihuacan, for already they held this great center of Mexican culture in awe and worship, and wished to copy from it. However, his wise old teacher taught him what a few of the great ones of the past had given to their special disciples as an inner secret—how to defend himself without hurting an enemy by moving with and using his power, and that of the inner power of the universe which each person has hidden within. So he was taught in daily exercise how to whirl in a circle like the whirlwind, to merge with a grasp or blow like the leaves of the willow merge with the wind, until the enemy went down and did not know how it had happened, or was held immobilized in a mysterious, painful grasp that yet did him no permanent harm.

"Be always calm," the old one taught him, "having neither fear nor anger, for both of these emotions destroy the true human spirit within you and turn you into a wild beast, either fleeing senselessly or raging and destroying. Let the power of the universe enter into your body and center there, flowing outward through every limb like a great river against which the might of the strongest man cannot prevail. So do you become one with all living things and with the earth and sky." And he learned also the ultimate secret, how to take a weapon from an armed man, even when he himself was unarmed, yet how to do it quickly and cleanly, like the experienced otter catching a fish.

Soon the boy grew into a youth, wonderful in physique, swift as the deer, supple as the ocelot, his eyes glowing with that love and curiosity that makes the true man. He it was that stopped boys from throwing sticks and stones at dogs or even snakes, whose eyes blazed when a small child was teased and bullied by a larger one, and whose hand and body moved quickly to end such tyranny. Towards girls he gave the honor, respect and protection that was due the future mothers-of-life, but those who sought to lure him with their subtle ways were answered with laughter and teasing until they realized ruefully he was strangely beyond pettiness and ephemeral attachments.

Into the silence of the wilderness, to the hilltops and the mountains, he went to pray and fast, as the *tlamatimime* had taught him, as he instinctively knew he should. One dawn on a mountain top he extended his arms to the sky and watched the coming of the daybreak star (Venus), and the glowing pulsing colors of the sunrise until his being answered the cry of the Spirit and he knew, in a burst of glory and amazement brought by a great vision, that he was the Lord of the Dawn, promised to his people, to awaken them and lead them to a higher life on this planet.

Now he was a man and as a man he went to claim his inheritance. North he went near Colhuacan on Lake Tezcoco (see Map No. 3), to meet his evil uncles, the usurpers of his father's kingdom, and there he was lured, as they thought, to a cliff above the lake from which his body could be hurled when they killed him. They were mighty men of war, plumed and armored, expert with the spear and the obsidian sword, sure this little play of death would be over quickly. The spear hissed through the air and the sword whistled, their dark faces grimaced with the lust to kill, but somehow the slender youth moved at just the right moment. Supple as the willow he whirled and caught each weapon one by one and, with a twist that seemed feather-light yet was as strong as the tiger's, threw their weapons over the cliff.

Even weaponless, the warrior uncles were fearsome and muscled like giants. With their hands alone they knew they could tear him to pieces. They closed on him, white teeth flashing in grim and leering smiles, their steel-fingered hands like claws. Still, somehow he slipped between them, avoiding by but an inch the grasping hands, whirling twice to right and left, the touch of his hands again feather-light, and the two powerful adversaries missed him. Through their own momentum and fury they one by one went tumbling down over the cliff, their roars of rage changing to screams of fright.

There were men who saw what had happened and reported the miracle, some overreacting with astonishment and imagination to explain they had seen two bolts of lightning from the sky gods come to strike the two evil brothers. But the word spread like a roaring fire, like birds carried on the wind of a hurricane. And the people knew instinctively that they had a new great king.

How did he consolidate his kingdom or empire? By love, by kindness, by such purity of heart that his fame fanned out like the light of the sun coming warm with the springtime into the cold north, and also by firmness and understanding, for he taught sacred laws and a way of life that entered into the inner hearts of many men. He taught them to pray to and worship the Great Lord behind the Rainbow with flowers, to use no idols or human sacrifice, to see in all the good gods of the past the reflection of the One Great Spirit, and to see in all the evil gods man's own foolish desires magnified—made completely unworthy when understood in the light of honor, justice, harmony and love.

One of the great signs of his tremendous influence, his glowing love, was the reversal of the flight of the Pipiles (see Map No. 2), the lost intellectuals, artisans, artists and nobles of the Teotihuacan culture. These people had fled south, like leaves blowing before a great wind, fleeing first from the crude warlike barbarian Chichimecs of the north, and then, diverting to a side, fleeing the tyrannical Olmecs who had come up from the south to capture the sacred city of Cholula (see Map No. 1).

Now many of them turned back toward the north again, hearing the good news of the wonderful king. So the *tlamatinime,* the wise ones or intellectuals and the ancient wise priests of Quetzalcoatl started the long trek first, for they knew the deeper meanings. Then the Nonoalca began to come. They also had wise priests and philosophers, but they numbered many of the most famous artisans of the past, experts in the art of working gold, copper, brass and mother of pearl, and at inlaying gems of jade and lapis-lazuli, fire opals and turquoise. Then there were the Amanteca, the master artists, the writers, drawers and painters of the sacred books, the codices, that bore the histories of the peoples, the makers of tapestries of living colors out of cotton, the creators of marvelous beauty.

Back from Huehuetlapallan and possibly even from Cotzaculaco at the Isthmus of Tehuantepec, all these people and many others who had heard of the new and glorious kingdom came. Traveling along the Gulf Coast to avoid the tyrannical Olmecs, they turned inland at Quiahuiztian and on through Zacatlan, Iztoc and Tollantzinco, a long and arduous journey through much danger, to reach the one they longed for at the new and brilliant city of Tollan (see Map No. 2).

Now indeed a city was made to dazzle and delight the eyes of men, a city dedicated to peace and harmony. Beautiful colored frescoes, often inlaid with precious minerals of many colors, covered the walls, while the terraces of all the buildings glowed with flowering shrubs and trees in which birds of many kinds sang and played. The birds even came into the houses of the people to sing to the delighted children, who were taught to treat them and all life with respect and love. Flower-decked boats and barges were rowed through the city's wide canals beneath the great pyramids of the sun and the moon on whose tops the Lord of the Universe was worshiped with glorious flowers and where no human sacrifice was allowed. So later people would sing of those wonderful Toltecs of the time of Ce Acatl Tolpiltzin Quetzalcoatl:

"The Toltecs were a skillful people;
all of their works were good, all were exact,
all well made and admirable.

Their houses were beautiful, with turquoise mosaics,
the walls finished with plaster,
clean and marvelous houses, which is to say,
Toltec houses, beautifully made,
beautiful in everything . . .

Painters, sculptors, carvers of precious stones,
feather artists, potters, spinners, weavers,
skillful in all they made; they discovered
the precious green stones, the turquoise;
they knew the turquoise and its mines;
they found the mountain hiding
silver and gold, copper and tin,
and the metal of the moon (platinum?).

The Toltecs were truly wise;
they conversed with their own hearts . . .
They played their drums and rattles;
they were singers, they composed songs
and sang them among the people;
they guarded the songs in their memories,
they deified them in their hearts.

(From the *Codice Matritense de la Real Academia VIII*, folio 172 r.-v.)

Over such gifted people Quetzalcoatl reigned with song and laughter, great wisdom and the thrill of the spirit. He formed the two orders of the

Jaguar Knights and the Eagle Knights, both members also of the Brotherhood of the Tree, and dedicated, as were the Knights of the Round Table of King Arthur, to the search for spiritual strength and to deeds of honor and mercy and kindness towards all the people of Mexico.

From Tollan and out to all corners of the empire and beyond to many other cities and nations traveled the merchant-missionaries, the *pochtecas,* teaching Quetzalcoatl's way of life while earning their way by trading and selling goods carried on their backs. They made good money sometimes from their work, but generally gave most of it away to help the poor and widowed, for to them the money was purely secondary to giving the Word of the Spirit. Thus an ancient poem of Chilam Balam, the great Mayan priest and seer, told of them:

"You are to wander,
entering and departing
from strange villages   .   .   .
Perhaps you will achieve nothing anywhere.
It may be your merchandise
and your items of trade
find no favor in any place   .   .   .
But do not turn back, keep a firm step   .   .   .
Something you will achieve;
Something the Lord of the Universe will assign to you   .   .   ."

(Taken from page 93 of *Mexican and Central American Mythology,* by Irene Nicholson, Hamilyn Publishing Group, 1967.)

Though some of the beautiful teachings of Quetzalcoatl were lost in the centuries that followed and warlike nations turned to idol-worship and human-sacrifice, the purity and goodness of his message comes through in these words of an Aztec father to his teen-age son:

"Do not throw yourself upon women
Like the dog which throws itself upon food.
Be not like the dog
When he is given food or drink,
giving yourself up to women before the time comes.
"Even though you may long for women,
Hold back, hold back with your heart!
   until you are a grown man, strong and robust.
Look at the maguey plant.
If it is opened before it has grown
And its liquid is taken out,
It has no substance.
It does not produce liquid; it is useless.

But, before it is opened
to withdraw its water,
it should be allowed to grow and attain full size.
Then its sweet water is removed all in good time.

This is how you must act;
before you know woman,
you must grow and be a complete man.
And then you will be ready for marriage;
You will beget children of good stature,
Healthy, agile, and comely.''

(From the text of *Codice Florentino,* Book VI, folio 97, r.)

Under Quetzalcoatl men and women alike were taught to become strong in heart and mind as well as in body, self-controlled and poised, masters of themselves, and by so doing, becoming great in spirit, regardless of their station in life. Thus it was said in those days:

''Even if he were poor and lowly,
even if his mother and his father were the poorest of the poor .   .   .
His lineage was not considered,
only his way of life mattered   .   .   .
The purity of his heart,
his good and humane heart   .   .   .
It was said that he had the Lord of Being in his heart,
that he was wise in the things of that Lord.

(From the *Florentine Codex,* Book III, folio 67.)

Those who truly believed in these teachings became members of the Fellowship of the Tree. What was this tree? From all which can be read about Quetzalcoatl, perhaps it could best be put into words like this:
   ''There is a great tree, which we call the Tree of Life and Understanding, a Sacred Tree that every tree we meet symbolizes, though those that are great and strong, with mighty branches and their roots deep in the earth so the wind does not bother them, symbolize it more strongly. Around this Tree is the Sacred Circle of our love and unity, which we symbolize by merging our hearts together and working to fulfill the teachings of the Great Creator. The Fellowship of the Tree means to turn a bright and shining face to the world, a face of kindness and love, of humbleness, purity and justice. Thus all men can trust us; thus all women and children are protected by us; thus the families flower in honor and respect; thus the nation grows in strength and goodness but without harming others; thus the plants and animals and birds are treated by us as brothers, used only when we really need them, and with

a prayer that Mother Earth may soon renew them. Keep the Brotherhood of the Tree and men will sing of this day when we walked in beauty. Someday the Mighty Tree will spread its branches over the whole earth, and men everywhere will walk in unity and harmony!"

Unfortunately, the beautiful world of the Toltecs under Quetzalcoatl, the priest-king-prophet, was not to last long. There were evil men who envied the shining face of Quetzalcoatl and his power over the people. His wisdom, firmness, kingship and vast prestige hindered their greed for wealth and power and their lust for women and gold. They were followers of Tetzcatlipoca, the dark god of the north, who had been twisted by men's thoughts into a monster, a lover of blood and violence and of other dark ways of the soul. They kept alive the same secret Jaguar Cults that once, by their selfishness and depravity helped bring down the early civilizations of the Maya and Teotihuacan. They were also extremely clever and knew the only thing which would turn the people against Quetzalcoatl. They waited a long time to recapture control, but when that time came they were ready.

So the darkness began to come back to Meso-America when Quetzalcoatl, the great king, became sick. There are some who suspect he was secretly poisoned. At this time of his sickness an old man came to the gate of the palace and asked to see the king, saying he had a special medicine to heal him. He was an innocent-looking old man with white hair, but he kept his eyes humbly down so nobody could see into them. Three times the guards of the palace tried to drive him away, but he was persistent and his voice rose until Quetzalcoatl, groaning in pain, heard him and ordered the guards to let him in.

The old man entered, bowed low, and spoke: "I have here, Lord, a liquid that is made from special roots and leaves that will relieve you of all your pain and make you well."

"No," said the king, "it looks suspicious to me. It may be poison!"

"It is not poisonous; it has a marvelous taste and will truly make you well. Try but a tiny bit of it and you will see what I mean."

The old man kept insisting that Quetzalcoatl try just a bit of it, just a taste, and finally he did.

It had a nice taste and almost instantly it made him feel better, so he took a few more sips. Each time he felt better and better, and he did not notice that as he continued to drink, he became increasingly unbalanced and tipsy. Finally, he became drunk, for the liquid contained the powerful fermented juice of a certain cactus. Soon his senses left him and he fell into a stupor.

No one really knows what happened to him while he was drunk, because his enemies now had him in their hands, and they used him to shock the people, claiming that in his drunken state he had committed several sins. Thus do the dark enemies of all that is beautiful work to destroy by poison, drink, prison, exile, torture or death those Shining Beings who seek to bring us the Light of the Great Spirit.

It was indeed a terrible shock to the Toltecs to see their famous king, so noted for his sobriety, purity and great nobility, now acting like any other drunken man, but it was also a time of great testing. Those whose adoration for their king was shallow, based only on surface appearances, now turned against him, shouting for his overthrow in a growing mob, but those who had really deeply savoured his beautiful spirit were broken-hearted that this dark thing had happened, but they realized his real self was only temporarily hidden. Some of these carried him away and hid his drunkenness until he recovered. When his senses returned and he began to realize what had happened, he was filled with terrible remorse and sorrow. He asked his friends what he had done while unconscious. They were afraid to tell him, not knowing for sure which of the things said about their king were only shouted lies and which the truth. In anguish and pennance for his sins, whatever they were, he thrust maguey thorns through his tongue and legs, causing them to bleed so that the blood and pain might wash away some of what he had done.

When he tried to talk again to the Toltecs, most would no longer listen to him, but shouted:

"Liar, thief, adulterer! Leave us before we kill you!"

Utterly saddened, yet strengthened by those who loved him, mostly members of the Nonoalca, the Amanteca, the *pochtecas* and the *tlmatinimes*—most of them philosophers, artisans, artists, traveling merchant-missionaries, and similar people who always had recognized his greatness—he left the beautiful city, traveling south. Soon he and the people with him reached the famous Valley of Mexico and the city of Cholula, at the time ruled by the historic Olmecs. The Olmecs apparently were afraid to bother him because of his great fame and let him stay in their city for several years, where again he pierced his legs and tongue in agony of mind over what had befallen him in Tollan. Slowly he healed and began to teach again. In this city of Cholula, later followers built great temples and pyramids in his honor.

Into the highest mountains of Mexico, along the slopes of the great volcanos he led his people, and here in the glorious summer they rested in the meadows, hunted among the forests and streams and renewed their spirit. But, unfortunately, from here on his trail becomes confused and dim. Some say most of the people were trapped that fall in a great snow storm of the mountains and many died, causing Quetzalcoatl great anguish. There are legends that he went south either into Yucatan or into Oaxaca, the land of the Zapotecs, and there at the ancient Tree of Life at El Tule, helped plan the wonderful city of Mitla, where grew a sacred library. Others say he sailed away on a serpent raft into the eastern sea, to a land of paradise beyond the horizon, promising to come back when the time was ripe. And some say that in the mountains he met four sacred disciples who drank deeply of his spirit and then took his teachings to the four corners of America. It is known that some of his followers did reach Yucatan and that either he, himself, or one of his great disciples was with them. It was probably the disciple called Gucamatz who had the same purity and spirit as Quetzalcoatl, and who came to be called Kukulkan, which in Mayan means "Feathered Serpent." These people, being peaceable and highly moral, appear to have been welcomed by the Maya and much of their religion was accepted. They helped build the famous holy city of Chichen Itza, the word "Itza" being possibly a Mayan word for these strangers who came to their land. Later this city joined with Mayapan and Uxmal to found the great League of Mayapan, which flourished for nearly two centuries. Then came a new wave of Toltec people out of the north, also called Itzas, but these were totally different from the first who came, and they brought with them all the bad that had come to Tollan after Quetzalcoatl left it, including human sacrifice, the worship of idols, and loose conduct between men and women. They also now came as conquerors. The Maya spoke of these latecomers as follows:

"They brought shameful things when they came. They lost their innocence in carnal sin. This was the cause of our sickness also. There were no more lucky days for us; we had no sound judgment. At the end of our loss of vision and of our shame everything shall be revealed. There was no great teacher, no great speaker, no supreme priest when the change of rulers occurred at their arrival. Lewd were the priests . . . " (From *The Book of Chilam Balam of Chumayel*, translated by Ralph E. Roys, University of Oklahoma Press, 1967.)

These invaders were in time overthrown and Maya rule again established, but things got even worse for the Maya a century or so later when the Spaniards came. Thus the same great Mayan scribe writes:

"Before the coming of the mighty men, the Spaniards, there was no robbery by violence, there was no greed and striking down one's fellow man in his blood, at the cost of the poor man, at the expense of the food of each and everyone. It was the beginning of tribute, the beginning of church dues, the beginning of strife with purse snatching, the beginning of strife by trampling of people, the beginning of robbery and violence, the beginning of debts enforced by false testimony, the beginning of individual strife, a beginning of vexation . . . "

No wonder the Indians called this "the beginning of the nine hells!"
And no wonder Chilam Balam wrote:

"On that day the first strutting turkey cocks (Spaniards) arrived. On that day there were whippings at Chakanputun. The people subsisted on trees; they subsisted on stones. When the invasion came—even the heavens pitied themselves!"

The very name "strutting turkey cocks" typifies the vanity and pride of the white men, when they considered themselves so much better than those they had conquered—the Maya, one of the gentlest and most civilized people in the history of the world! How sad that the Spaniards should feel the cutting power of the sword of greater worth than the love and respect the Lord of Us All asks be used in dealings with each other! How much indeed had the self-styled Christians of that time fallen away from the teachings of Jesus, even as the Toltecs fell away from the teachings of Quetzalcoatl.

But Quetzalcoatl promised that one day he would come back. This is similar to the promise of Jesus and to the promises of some other great prophets and culture heroes. Does this necessarily mean the return of the same person or persons? Or could it as well mean the return of the same beautiful spirit and teaching, but in the body and mind of another Sacred Teacher of Mankind?

chapter TEN

Out of the
Silence They
Also Came Singing

They sing:

"The Ulikron, Ngobo Ulikron (orphan of the virgin), traveled from the north, the far, far north, the cold, cold north. He talked to stout little men, to tall red men, to men in huts, to men in tall houses made of stone, to men who make broad roads and wear fine soft clothes, and pearls and silver and gold, to men who look like the sun in their dress and wisdom and might. Yes, the Ulikron passed among them long, long ago and told the men to be good, to do good, to love good. The Ulikron passed and talked; the Ulikron was lovely; his eyes were soft and seeing; his eyes saw through men; the Ulikron's eyes saw and saw and saw, and men looked on and wept and stopped their wars; they stopped their hate; their bows and arrows shot the deer, but never man again; and long they walked the Ulikron Way and talked of him till one great chief began to war again and build big houses of stone. Yes, the Ulikron went down to the end of the earth. He went to the far south and talked. He saw the land of gold and the land of great waters and the great stone houses and men dressed in gold and soft clothes who built long roads—men of great wisdom born of the stars.

"The Ulikron pointed to the stars. He talked of the Meselen (the Crab), the Tolen (the Plough), and the Men (the Great Bear). He talked of the God above those stars, and he told men to be good and that He would come again for all good men; and men began to be good.

"All Indians wait for the Ulikron!"

From a legend of the Guaymi Indians of Panama, given in *A Guaymi Grammar and Dictionary, with some Ethnological Notes,* by Ephraim S. Alphones, Smithsonian Institution, Bureau of American Ethnology, Bulletin 162.

UPON FIRST READING THE ABOVE description of the Ulikron, it was immediately apparent that this obviously very spiritual person must have been the source of the knowledge and power of Chio Jari since the latter was a Mountain Guaymi. But while I was in Panama, many of the lower country Guaymi had fallen far away from the beautiful teachings of their culture hero, the Ulikron. For example, their great stick games and dances, which once were spiritual and good before they became contaminated by white civilization, had degenerated into drunken orgies. Dozens of traders came up from the lowlands to these dances loaded with alcoholic drinks to trade for anything of value the Indians had. Under the influence of the alcohol all spiritual thoughts and all moral standards were forgotten! Happily, of late, the word is that things are gradually changing for the better now with these people.

Great Central American culture heroes

It is possible that the Guaymi Ulikron was simply the local name for Quetzalcoatl or one of his great disciples, such as Gucamatz, who came south in Central America with the same inspired message. What makes this seem likely is the Guaymi account that the Ulikron came from the Far North. Or it could have been a still different other unique human being, a messenger from the Great Spirit, but one of a different time and place. His very exceptional spiritual power and nature seems quite obvious from the words: "his eyes were soft and seeing; his eyes saw through men; the Ulikron's eyes saw and saw and saw, and men looked on and wept and stopped their wars; they stopped their hate." Such a being all people should be glad to see again!

The Cuna Indians of Eastern Panama (part of whom are called the San Blas) have a similar legend of a creat culture hero. His name was Ipeorkun Kunkilel, a name pronounced so much like the name Ulikron as to be thought of as simply the Cuna translation of the name of the same person. He was also called "The Golden One descended from the Sun," who taught the people how to heal the sick, to develop the powers of a wise seer, to follow a high moral law, and to know about a beautiful heaven where the good would go. He lived on earth about fifty years, the Cuna say, and also taught hospitality, kindness and helpfulness to one another, and especially to the aged, the widows and the orphans, as part of the way to serve God.

It is interesting that many of these culture heroes are called children of virgins (Quetzalcoatl and Sweet Medicine, too, for example). Some people have claimed that this was picked up since the coming of Christianity to America, and that the Native Americans simply copied the idea for their own culture heroes. This is quite possible, of course, though there is clear evidence of old books about Quetzalcoatl that the idea of children born of virigin mothers was asserted long before the whites came. In fact, long before the coming of Jesus there were stories and legends among the Old World peoples, too, of the virgin births of such culture heroes as Hercules, Krishna, Zoroaster and so on. Perhaps it is natural for men everywhere to assume that their great religious heroes had special divine births, to account for their abilities to speak and act with superhuman spiritual power, insight and love.

Usually such figures appear when they are most needed, those times of darkness in human affairs when old religions have become corrupt or divided and mankind in different parts of the world has become selfish, warlike and without moral standards. How gloriously they bring back that which was lost, yet how sad it is that many people fight against or reject them.

God-like beings who came to the peoples of western South America

Often there is no clear line between the culture hero and the sky God—or one of the sky gods. Thus Quetzalcoatl was called the God of the Morning Star and even the Creator of Life in some legends. Similarly, the people of Peru and Bolivia recall that in very ancient times there came to them a man of divine nature called "Con Ticci Viracocha," who is sometimes called in legends "the World Maker", and he is also spoken of as a man who walked the earth and taught people to love one another and to be good and kind. Some say he came from the South and others from the North, and some say he was a white man, which is one reason probably that the Incas at first welcomed their Spanish conqueror, Pizarro, as if he were a white god, until they found out too late that he and his men brought much sorrow.

Viracocha also destroyed evil men, it is said, and taught the people many arts of civilization. Once, they say, when he was attacked by the

Canas tribe, he caused a mountain to blaze with fire and the Canas fell down and worshiped him. After teaching many good things, he went away by sea, disappearing into the west and was not seen again, though it was promised that he would come back. This voyage into the west Thor Heyerdahl tried to duplicate on his great raft Kon Tikki, a trip that also proposed to show that South Americans once sailed west and added to the civilization and culture of the South Sea Islanders.

Another culture hero of this area, who is described sometimes as an old man with a beard, was called Thunupa (also Tonapa and Taapac), though this may be simply another name for Viracocha, possibly at a different stage in his life. Such beards, by the way, often in the old days among the Indians of North, South and Central America, were supposed to be worn only by holy beings. Thunupa was both loving and kind to good people and harsh and violent to bad people, whom he often destroyed or turned into stone. The natives will still point these out to visitors. The Spaniards thought he might have been one of the Christian saints who somehow came to America, such as Saint Thomas or Saint Bartholomew, but it could as well be assumed that the vanity of the white men did not allow them to admit that the Indians could have ever had equivalent holy beings of their own!

It is said that Thunupa came from the North with five disciples. He told the people to stop their drinking that led to drunkenness, to marry and be true to just one wife, and to stop their wars. His enemies tried to destroy him and some of his disciples were cruelly martyrd, but Thunupa escaped in a magic raft that carried him across Lake Titicaca without oars. He continued to wander about the land and preached against the stone idols, which he often destroyed. But it is not clear what happened to Thunupa in the end.

The name Viracocha was taken by one of the greatest of the Inca emperors, who tried to emulate in his life that of the famous culture hero. His father had been a weak and vacillating man who nearly led the Empire into ruins, but Viracocha bravely undertook to defeat the enemies of the Incas, and restore the power and prestige of the Divine King. After his father died, the reign of Viracocha was a long and good one in which he was kind and forgiving, even to his enemies, and he set the standard of accepting conquered peoples into the Empire on the basis of equality and justice. It was probably his influence and that of the earlier Viracocha, which kept the Incas from becoming the same kind of cruel conquerors as the Aztecs who cut out the hearts of thousands of war captives in tribute to their war and sun god.

One of the strangest acts of the Emperor Viracocha was to build a special temple dedicated to the sun. Within it was a special chamber in which he caused two statues of bearded men to be carved. He promised that these two men would one day come to help the world become united and in harmony. This was one reason the Incas later accepted the Spaniards at first as divine beings, until they were very quickly and rudely proved mistaken! It is interesting that the Maya, in the famous Book of Chilam Balaam of Tizimin, speaks of "two bearded ones", who would be sacred beings, coming from the East to unite the world.

North of the Incas were a civilized people of many small kingdoms, called the Chibchas of what is now the country of Columbia. Their culture hero had one of the longest names of all and was called Nemterequeteba, but he also had other names, such as Sugomonxe, Sugunsua (the person who can disappear), Bochica (meaning person of the sun), and Chimzapagua. They say he came out of the east (from what is now Venezuela) into Columbia, about fourteen hundred years before the coming of the Spaniards. This would put him closer to the time of the *first* Quetzalcoatl rather than the second (later one), mentioned in Chapter Nine.

This was probably a time when the Chibcha were still a tribal folk and had rather recently learned how to grow corn, beans and squash. Nemterequeteba traveled over the country as an old man with long hair and a long beard, teaching the people chastity, clean-mindedness, kindness and helpfulness of conduct, urging them to give up all drunkenness and other self-indulgence, while learning the useful arts of spinning, weaving and painting textiles. One story says he lived for a while in a cave near the town of Cota, where he was protected from the large crowds that came to see him by a stone parapet, from which he preached. He organized a new religion, with priests who were taught to lead lives of purity and help the people. When this job was done he mysteriously disappeared.

There is some evidence that after Nemterequeteba most of the Chibchas became united and created a lively civilization, but by the time of the coming of the Spaniards, they had broken up into numerous small city states at war with each other, making them easy to conquer. A symbol of the Chibchas' fall from grace was the goddess Huitaca, who was supposed to have come to the Chibchas later than Nemeterequeteba. She taught them just the opposite way of life, including drunkenness and all forms of self-indulgence. Possibly they invented her as a good excuse for doing what they wanted to do and so forgot the good teachings of the culture hero who had once united and civilized them.

An unusual culture hero—Chinigchinix of Southern California

Chinigchinix (also called Chinigchinich, Changichnish, etc.) came to the Indians of Southern California at what must have been a fairly recent time, that is, not long before the coming of the Spaniards. He taught a religion of aggressive missionary activity, trying to convert different tribes. There is evidence that this missionary work had brought the religion very definitely to such tribes as the Tongva (Gabrieleño), Atahum (Luiseño), and Iviatim (Cahuilla); at least partially to the Chumash of the Santa Barbara area, and the Kamia (Diegueño) of the San Diego area; and possibly to the Salinan Indians of the Salinas Valley and the Yokuts of the San Joaquin Valley.

The story of Chinigchinix comes to us mainly through the eyes and writing of a Father G. Boscana, a Franciscan Father in Southern California early in the 19th century. It is fortunate for history there was this man who opened his mind and used his curiosity to investigate and tell about these tribal peoples, for very little is otherwise left of their culture or onetime presence. Although he had much difficulty in penetrating the wall of secrecy with which the Indians naturally surrounded their sacred things from the conquering whites, he tried his best to make friends with them.

Father Boscana was not sure where Chinigchinix came from, but there is some evidence he was born on Santa Catalina Island, about 30 miles out in the Pacific from the Southern California Coast, an island which had been occupied by the Tongva or Gabrieleño Indians for some centuries. The whole culture of this area was a unique and beautiful one, in which Shoshone language-speaking peoples (such as the Cahuila, Tongva, etc.) had come from the East perhaps a thousand years ago and driven a wedge to the ocean, separating the Hokan-Speaking Chumash of Santa Barbara County from the Hokan-speaking Kamia or Diegueño of San Diego County. The Shoshonean invaders gradually picked up the artistic and technical arts of the Chumash and the Kamia. The whole area was noted for the beautiful plank canoes, their boards split from logs by bone, horn and rock wedges and malls, then made leakproof with the aid of pitch and oil from seepages on the coast. These light, bouyant canoes were handled with extreme speed and skill by their Indian navigators, astonishing the Spanish with the way they dashed in circles about the clumsy Spanish ships. With these canoes they could fish in the open ocean and visit far outlying islands such as Santa Catalina, Santa Cruz and Santa Rosa. Most of these peoples took the soft stone, called soap stone or steatite, and carved it into beautiful forms of birds, animals and humans, the Chumash being particularly good at this art and also at producing most exquisite full-color paintings on cave walls.

To all these people Chinigchinix brought a religion of high moral standards, including the concept of eventual punishment for misdeeds.

This must have struck the early Catholic missionaries in the area as very similar to their own teachings of Hell as punishment. The difference, however, was that Chinigchinix promised a hell right in this life whenever anyone broke the laws he taught. It would come, he said, through sickness or by attack, particularly at night, of dangerous animals or demons, this last for especially bad people. Evidently Chinigchinix made his promises of punishment very convincing, because Father Boscana reported that almost all the people tried very hard to be good and very few broke the rules. He also said that lying, stealing and promiscuous sex relations were practically unknown among these peoples and their family life was very close and strong.

Perhaps Chinigchinix had to use strong fear of punishment because he had come to an area which had been under the grip of the Coyote shamans for many generations. These people used their spiritual powers largely for evil. They poisoned their enemies, or used the threat of poison and/or evil spirits to get their way. The religion of Chinigchinix sought to overcome the power of these shamans or to change their ways over a period before the Spaniards arrived. Of course, new shamans evolved within the Chinigchinix religion, too.

There were two rather unique features of this new religion, though there was a possibility both may have been used before the time of Chinigchinix. One was the use of a vision-producing drink, taken from the thorn apple (genus *Datura*). This drink, called by many of the Indians, Taloache, was made from the ground-up plant and administered to boys at the time of their initiation into manhood accompanied by a period of prolonged ceremonial dancing. This drugged the boys into a deep sleep, from which most of them awoke with claims of visions of some animal or natural force, like the thunder or rainbow, that would be their guardian spirits. The guardian spirits were to be of help to them all their lives, but Chinigchinix had evidently tied it also to the idea of leading a good moral life. Evidence of this is in the sandpainting which ended the ceremonial period. The sandpainting—usually by an old man, probably a shaman—was very important in showing each boy his relationship to the Great Spirit, to all life, and to his family and tribelet. The painting usually featured a large circle with smaller circles of the sun and moon inside, indicating the whole universe, and with the forms of different animals, reptiles, birds, etc. to indicate the forms of life with which the Indian was intimately involved.

Both boys and girls might be taught about life and religion at these sandpainting sessions in which the old leaders talked to them and impressed them with the sacred duty to live in the right way for the benefit of themselves, their families and people by being in harmony with the Great Spirit and His creations. They were also taught to pray at regular intervals each day to get spiritual strength and to resist temptations. The boys were warned over and over of the evil that would come to them if they broke the laws. There was practically no juvenile delinquency because all the teen-agers knew the true stories of boys who had made the mistake of thinking they could forget the teachings of their elders, and who had been turned on suddenly by the tribelet and killed. The girls also were very strictly guarded and taught how to preserve their purity so they could enter into marriage in a sacred way, give good teachings with a whole heart to their children, and thus preserve the honor of the family and the tribe.

Opposite the terrible punishment that might strike them if they broke the rules, all the people were promised by Chinigchinix that a paradise lay beyond the rainbow over the western sea, a place where good people would find great happiness after death. It was, indeed, as even Father Boscana had to admit, a very strong religion in which the promise of reward for good deeds and punishment for bad deeds was made very real for young and old alike.

Some shadowy figures out of legends who might have been culture heroes

In the legends of many peoples in North, South and Central America, there are stories of dimly-perceived gods or heroes of the past who could likely have been real men or women, real culture heroes who worked to change for the better the hearts and minds of the Native Americans, but whose messages and natures are seen only in part or dimly through the mists of time.

Such a one was Kuksu, "the hero god from the south", who came, so legend tells us, first to the Wintun people who lived on the western side of the Sacramento Valley in California and its east-facing mountain slopes. He either brought or the people developed somehow from his teachings a secret religious society called the "Kuksu Cult." This cult spread from the Wintun to neighboring tribes such as the Maidu, the Miwok, Pomo and Wappo, including most of the peoples of the Sacramento Valley, the surrounding mountains and the North-Central Coast. Down through the centuries the cult broke into two major divisions, divided by the main crest of the coast range. It became complicated by new ceremonies in the large and culturally rich valleys, and in some places it even lost touch with the name "Kuksu."

More important than trying to understand these complications, all described in various books, one needs only to try to understand how the cult affected the people. While it is not possible to do it in all cases, of course, thinking about and comparing these effects with earlier concepts and teachings, particularly where they are seen to be remarkably similar, suggests that the effects may very reasonably be linked to the earlier profound influence of a specific culture hero.

During the ceremonies much dancing was done, and they culminated with the appearance of spirit impersonators, including one very elaborately dressed to impersonate Kuksu, whether so named or not. Beautiful bark, feather, skin and tule costumes were worn. Basic to the ceremonies was the initiation of boys and girls into manhood and womanhood, the boys into the secret society to which all the adult males of the tribe (or tribelet) eventually belonged. In these proceedings the initiates were put under piles of leaves and branches and scarred with sharp sticks on their backs as part of the ordeal, the boys particularly, to prepare them for the courage needed in manhood. Later the ash demons came, men painted and disguised with ashes, who acted like clowns but who had the serious job of teaching the boys they must have respect for their elders, and boys who had shown too much skepticism or discourtesy were sometimes literally tossed through a roaring fire. At the very end of the ceremonies healing of sick people by the impersonators was done as part of the dance. After this the wise old men or chiefs gave talks about the laws of life and the spirit and how the young people must live to become truly good members of the tribelet. The ideal person was sober, industrious, loyal in marriage, pure-hearted, kind and obedient to the elders and chiefs who directed activities. It seems reasonably probable that these teachings did come originally from the one named Kuksu.

Not all was perfect in these northern California communities for there were some shamans who frequently tried to use their powers to control, fleece or even kill others by magic. Poisoners and Bear Doctors (people who dressed up as bears and used the impersonation to frighten others for their own designs) were found among the Pomo, for example. They were opposed by the chiefs and good shamans, and sometimes killed outright when caught at scurrilous business.

The Navajos and Apaches have closely related languages, so apparently were one people long ago who wandered down out of what is now Canada, where they lived with other Athabascan-speaking tribes between five and ten centuries ago. They have similar stories of one or more culture heroes, but these are pictured more as monster and demon slayers rather than as givers of moral laws.

The twin heroes of the Apaches were called Child-of-the-Waters and Killer-of-Enemies, but the latter is sometimes spoken of as an older brother or even the father of Child-of-the-Waters, who was born from White-painted Woman, actually the earth goddess or Mother Earth. In any case, Child-of-the-Waters is by far the greatest of these heroes, even as Slayer-of-Enemy-Gods is the main hero of the Navajos.

Coyote came before these heroes, as both the bringer of fire to men and also as the creator of trouble for them. Lust, lying, thieving, self-ishness, power-seeking, gluttony, greed—all were tried first by Coyote and then let loose by him among men. In fact, among some tribes, Coyote can be thought of as both good and evil, gladly contributing to our strength or to our weakness, whichever we let him do. Indeed, a very accommodating being is Coyote!

The monsters that Child-of-the-Waters slays or conquers have their powers turned for the betterment of man in many accounts, and Child-of-the-Waters joins with his mother, White-painted Woman, to teach the Apaches their Adolescent Girls Ceremony, in which the purity of the girl or woman is taught.

These facts make it possible to picture Child-of-the-Waters as a culture hero who counteracts the bad influence of Coyote, thereby giving moral teachings to the Apaches. Since such high teachings as chastity, honesty, service to others, and spiritual prayers were taught to Apache young people in the old days, it is possible to assume that there was a man—a culture hero but one who later became thought of as a god—who came with these teachings. The same could be said of the culture hero of the Navajos, the Slayer-of-Alien-Gods. With very little else known about them, the whole story must be left to conjecture.

Among some of the outlying tribes, far from the civilized centers of the Native Americans, are stories of men who came as transformers, for example, changing bad people into rocks or fish and helping good people get spiritual strength. These legends are similar to the stories of Child-of-the-Waters and Kuksu, as the transformers are thought of as being more god-like than man.

Such a being is Carancho, a folk hero of the Toba and Pilaga Indians of the Gran Chaco in what is now Paraguay, South America. Carancho is pictured as a god-like man who teaches the Indians how to make hunting weapons, but he also teaches the animals how to flee and hide so they will be hard to find and kill. This seems a paradox until re-garded as a conservation design, since animals and birds too easily killed would soon be wiped off the face of the earth. He also taught the tribes the use of tobacco in ceremonies, and he is said to have cured the first man bitten by a rattlesnake, but evidence is lacking that he at the same time taught the Indians their moral code. So he does not qualify as a genuine culture hero and deserves only brief mention.

The transformer of the Plateau tribes of British Columbia, Canada, was a similar hero. He transformed bad people into rocks or fish, and helped good people in various ways, such as showing them methods of hunting or of weaving baskets, but nothing links him with the development of any moral code.

Similar, perhaps, is the Coyote Prophet of inland areas of Washington and Idaho. He is supposed to have left a great prophecy of the coming of two other prophets to unite the earth. This is carved on the rocks at Buffalo Eddy, twenty miles south of Clarkson, Washington, on the West bank of the Snake River.

The patterns of the culture heroes

From the practical standpoint, we have dealt enough now with culture heroes, though there are undoubtedly many more of these mentioned in legends of other tribes. But what has been given here seems surely enough to reveal a widespread pattern or series of patterns throughout the Americas of the comings long ago of very unusual and dynamically spiritual human beings who awakened the consciences of their peoples and led them to higher standards of conduct. One variation of the patterns is seen in the coming of such culture heroes as Degandawidah and Quetzalcoatl, at those times when mankind was most submerged in war, hate, disharmony, greed and the other weaknesses of human flesh. The culture hero turns them back from this dark path and, when he succeeds, the people "walk in beauty", as the Navajo sing in many of their songs.

Another pattern is that often the culture hero promises that he or one like him will return again when the world gets dark and the earth needs a Light-bringer. Is not all this evidence suggestive that the Great Spirit has a Great Plan, that He has helped mankind in all parts of the world, as a kind Father should and would, and is preparing them for a day of unity, beauty, honor and glory when the dark doings of man shall fade away before the blinding light of a New Teacher?

chapter ELEVEN

A Sioux Youth Prepares Himself for a Vision

"I circle around, I circle around
The boundaries of the earth,
Wearing the long wing-feathers as I fly."

A Ghost Dance song of the Arapaho, from page 950 of *The Ghost Dance Religion*, by James Mooney, 14th Annual Report of the Bureau of Ethnology, 1892-93.

IN MANY VISITS TO THE various Sioux reservations I have talked with some wonderful men and women who, as Crazy Horse foretold in his prophecy of the future, "would still mirror in their eyes the earth and sky." One Sioux lady told me: "When I was a little girl there were many more like that, for they still remembered the old way. As a child I felt so safe and protected around them and surrounded by love, for all children were thought of as the children of the Great Spirit and as being the future of the tribe."

It should be understood that many Native Americans in the old days found or felt that one vision was all they needed. At the time of this vision they made usually a small packet to wear around their neck that they called their "medicine bag." In this bag they would place things that reminded them of the tremendous experience of the vision and that would help them pray daily with renewed power to keep their minds and hearts pure so that the vision would continue to give them spiritual power all their lives. Others, however, would keep seeking for visions, trying to find those that would give them even greater power. Thus some visions seekers would go out for a vision search nearly every year or even oftener. The famous Sioux holy man, Crazy Horse, sought such frequent visions because he was so worried about the future of his people and sought visions to help them.

Those tribes who had a strong remembrance of their culture heroes, as the Sioux did of White Buffalo Calf Maiden, and the Cheyennes of Sweet Medicine, have approached their vision searches with a strong feeling of giving themselves in service to others and a deep seeking to obey the will of the Great Spirit.

Among most of the Plains tribes practically every young man and many a young woman was sent out to seek a vision, and this was true also in most of the Plateau and Eastern forest tribes. In effect their whole childhood was programmed to fill them with a desire to seek and receive visions, spirit power and an understanding of the sacrifice and ordeal involved. Most expected to contact one or more guardian spirits, usually seen in vision in the form of an animal or bird, or as a natural force like thunder and lightning. This guardian spirit, who was really a reflection of the Great Spirit in each seeker, would be with him all his life to help and protect him, especially if he kept his heart purified.

Even though most tried quite hard to find visions, many failed, but they would keep trying and trying. Among the Crow, Blackfeet and some other tribes, it was possible to purchase a vision from some other man, especially from one who had had many visions, but usually a vision could be passed on only to one who was worthy of it. Such a passed-on vision, however, was rarely considered as strong as one that had been received directly.

Today many Native Americans, both men and women and especially in the West, are seeking vision help by using peyote, a vision-producing cactus from Mexico, as part of the Native American Church. From experience and talks with many peyote-users, I have an impression that they have often been helped spiritually by this plant, but mainly only when it has been used ceremonially and correctly with great reverence. Perhaps it can be looked on as a crutch that has helped many Indian people rise above their spiritual despondence and estrangement since their conquest. A crutch is always a vital necessity when one is injured, but when one becomes well and strong again the rigorous physical, mental and spiritual discipline found in the old-time vision-search should bring help of greater and truer spiritual power. Peyote may be an easier way to find visions, but easier ways are not always the best ways.

Possibly one reason why so many even in the old days did not receive visions was because their cry for a vision was too selfish. Thus I heard of one man who asked: "Old Man, hear me; give me power over my enemies, make me live long, help my hunting, make me successful with women, help me have many horses!" Perhaps some who prayed this way did receive help, but how much more worthwhile would have been a prayer to the Spirit, asking help not for oneself, but for one's people or even all mankind?

Among many tribes in the old days there were both men and women who were looked up to as holy beings for the unselfish way they lived. They were people who devoted themselves to service to the tribe and to others. They healed the sick and comforted the broken-hearted or lonely; they brought food to the hungry, and gave horses to the poor. Essentially they had forgotten themselves and dedicated themselves to the Great Spirit. Such a one was Crazy Horse, also Black Elk, Ice of the Cheyennes, Plenty Coups of the Crow, Chief Joseph of the Nez Perce, Whirlwind Chaser and Elk Head.

These people were pointed out to the boys and girls and held up as examples for them to follow. If a young person seeking a vision came to one of these spiritual persons he would be given advice on how to seek a vision. It would go somewhat as we can now imagine an old wise one, Sees-beyond-the-Lightning, giving while talking to a young man still carrying his childhood name, Dawn Boy:

"Seeking power from the Above Ones is not a one-way path. You must give of yourself as the sun gives his light to the earth, as the cloud gives rain to the plants. It is also like following an antelope across the prairie by finding the marks of his hoofs. Only the good hunter can keep to such a trail, one whose eyes are alert for every little sign, such as the grass blade bowing up again after it has been struck to the ground. But when the best of hunters loses the trail in hard ground or on rocks, he can still follow it with his spirit if he lets his spirit enter into the spirit of the animal and so knows how it is feeling and where it wants to go.

"So do you let your spirit merge with the Spirits of the Powers of Sky and Earth, feeling as they are feeling, doing as they wish you to do, for they speak with the Voice of Wakan Tanka, the Lord of us All, and they will enter you in vision if they see the way open. Be then like a flute through which the breath blows unobstructed because your every thought is purified from the desires of men, and your desire is to be one with the Great Ones. Thus you begin purifying yourself months before the Inipi Ceremony in the Sweat-lodge, for this ceremony is only the final purification before you make your vision search and there is a long trail yet ahead for you before you enter that lodge.

"Seek lonely places and be still, listening, listening, hearing the songs and cries of the winged ones, the sounds of the four-leggeds and even the cries of the insect people; feeling, feeling, feeling the breath and touch of the earth, of leaves, of bark; for all have messages for you from the Above One. They are His creations and they talk to you sometimes with His voice.

"Be silent and motionless as the stone while you purify your spirit. Do you think it is easy? No, never! For the mind of man is like the dust that scatters in the breeze or dashes off in the whirlwind. Now bear down on your mind as you do with the arrow when you are straightening it. Hold and straighten your thoughts on the red road of purity that leads to the Great Spirit. Think what He has put you on earth for, that you might serve Him and serve your people, not to be a slave to your passions. A man who follows his own desires and lusts, or who lies and steals goes down in the spirit like the swallow who has been struck by lightning, or like the rabbit pierced by a hundred arrows.

"Think how the girls and women are sacred beings, sacred to the Great Spirit, dedicated to giving forth beautiful life, raised with honor in the circle of the family. Even to think of touching them without honor is to break the circle of the spirit and do harm to both you and them and possibly to many generations. Think and feel high, never low. See about you how beautiful are the rainbow, the sunset, the waterfall, the dawn, and see in the woman the same sacredness. See the otter who mates for life and is loyal to his mate to the death. Let your thoughts fly high like the eagle into the deep blue, and never let them creep low like the mole!

"So in the dawn you must pray for purity, for the circle of the roundness, for the growth of the Tree of Life, and for the life of your people and of all creatures that you may be one with them. Pray also at noon, and at the sunset and when you go to bed, and let your prayers rise like the smoke rises from our fires, freed from the earth, freed from all selfish desires till the Above One knows your heart is open and ready for the Gift of Power. And be content with what He gives you, for what He gives you, you will have earned and no more!"

Now the young man, Dawn Boy, stands up, after listening. His eyes lift to the blue skies and his body straightens like an arrow, poised to be fired into the heavens. He has heard the rhythm of those words, spoken with deep yearning that his heart may be touched, and has looked into those old dark eyes filled with wisdom. He has known what every Indian youth knew in those days, that one can never come back to those wise and piercing eyes after a vision search and look into them and tell a lie!

"There is one more thing to say," says Sees-beyond-the-Lightning, "and that is that before you can make your vision search and fast without food and water for whatever days it needs, you must strengthen your body until all your muscles and the blood that waters them sing with power. So learn to run up that hill over there until you can run without panting, and try chasing an antelope on foot till you cover the distance between those two streams [pointing] without stopping. Then learn to run in the night with spirit eyes, for this comes to you when your heart is pure and you let go of your thoughts and emotions as the bird lets go of the earth and springs into the blue. To do this right you must put your trust in the Above One. Try until it works, for you will fall down at first and be tempted to give up, but the one who keeps trying, and ever-strengthening the spirit, finally learns to let his spirit take over the body and direct it where the mind alone must fail. And take that big rock there and learn to throw it a little farther each day until you can lift and throw that bigger one over there. So will you grow strong in body as you also grow strong in the spirit and, when the time is ripe, we will have the Inipi, the Purification Ceremony. Go now, and may your heart be as the eagle, and your thoughts as the rainbow, pure, pure, and dedicated to your people!"

So Dawn Boy runs off to the hills and the old man follows his running with watchful eyes, yet filled with love and yearning, for he remembers when he was a youth and eager to be tried by the spirit. But the youth feels the caress of the breeze on his brown skin and the warm touch of the sunlight. The song of the meadowlark he hears with ears that read into every lilting warble the Voice of the Spirit, and all the earth seems to sing to him like a great orchestra tuning up for a major performance, and he knows with all his heart and soul that the Great One Above and all the Sacred Beings of earth and sky are watching him.

When such a spirit is one with its surroundings, climbing a hill very soon becomes an effortless running into the sky, and throwing a large rock becomes like tossing a ball. Days passed into weeks and, when the boy's muscles and blood sang within him as the Old One had told him they should, Dawn Boy came once more to the holy one and exclaimed:

"I have done what you said, and I am ready!"

Then Sees-beyond-the-Lightning stared long into his eyes and saw that he had told the truth. So quick was the test to the seeing eye. Out of the silence the wind sang through the pine needles, and far away a Red-tailed Hawk gave his wild and plaintive cry. Still the old one was silent, listening. When he had picked up the silent vibrations sought with his spirit ear, he reached out his hand and touched the young man.

"Tomorrow," he says, "we will have the Inipi Ceremony in the Sweat Lodge."

Let us put aside our lack of understanding of these matters for a moment and realize that this purification ceremony is a very sacred matter, especially when done by one of these holy ones. Everything is done with the utmost reverence, for the maker of the ceremony is calling together all the powers of earth and sky, and concentrating them so that out of this centering may come the very Essence of Wakan-Tanka Himself, the Lord of all Being. Everything about it has deep meaning, and it is up to the young man who attends this ceremony to purify himself for the Hanblecheyapi—the vision quest—and to be extraordinarily alert and soak in all these meanings. Only thus can he clear his mind and heart of all external things, of all earthly desires and thoughts, so his own being becomes a clear channel through which the breath of the spirit may blow. In this ceremony, as well as in the vision search, he is dedicating body, mind and soul for the rest of his life in service to his people and to Wakan-Tanka. In somewhat the same way the great Jewish and Christian saints and prophets went into the wilderness to seek spiritual help and prepare themselves for the ordeal of meeting and overcoming evil.

When the day dawned for the Inipi Ceremony, the clouds were playing across the blue sky with the wind, and the wind was also playing with the emerald grasses of the Great Plains, ruffling them and making them shimmer in long quivering lines of light as far as the eye could see. In those days the earth and sky were still untouched by the ugly hands of pollution and destruction, and the air was so clear it seemed you could see for a thousand miles! Also the water gurgling down the nearby creek and laughing over the stones was like liquid crystal. But the old ones knew a bad time was coming, with dark storms out of the east, with the coming of a strange people, and that there would be darkness and ugliness for some time before the light came again (see the prophecies in Chapter Fifteen). This is why they concentrated so much on reaching the young ones with the spirit so that at least a few would live to pass on to their grandchildren the precious spark of true life.

The old man, Sees-beyond-the-Lightning, had already chosen those who would share in the Inipi Ceremony with the young man, and they were now gathered at the sweat lodge. The fire outside was placed about ten feet from the opening to the lodge and faced the east, from where wisdom comes, and the fire was called "Peta-owihankeshi", meaning "the fire of no end." It thus symbolizes the eternal fire of the spirit that is ever kept kindled by the Great Spirit. Soon Sees-beyond-the-Lightning began to speak:

"We have made all things here holy (wakan) that we may be surrounded by pure thoughts and prepare ourselves for pure deeds. The fire we make here represents the great power of Wakan Tanka, which we can use ourselves either for good or evil, even as we can use our thoughts and our deeds either for good or evil. The rocks we put in the fire to heat up for the sweat bath represent the everlasting strength of Wakan-Tanka, and the steam that rises from them symbolizes the purifying power of their spirit, while the water also purifies because it is not only the softest and lowest thing we find, but also the most powerful because it can wear away even rock. So we should be humble and soft like the water, yet also strong and powerful as both rock and water. The willow trees from which the sweat lodge is built represent the tree people and all green growing things, and like them we should grow in beauty and strength, but also always able to renew our spirit even as they renew their leaves in the springtime.

"The roof of the sweat lodge is made from the skins of our brothers the buffalo, and so represents them whom Wakan Tanka has given to us as our chief food, but also symbolizes all the other animals, and the circle of the sky with its star people and winged people, all of whom must be purified in order to come before Wakan Tanka. The earth itself, on which we walk, represents Mother Earth, who gives us the bounty of many good things, and yet humbly lets us walk upon her, teaching us how to be humble and yet strong. The frame of the sweat lodge is made to show the four quarters of the universe, so that the lodge is like an image of the complete universe, with the hot stones in the center being the place where Wakan Tanka resides, and all the two-leggeds, four-leggeds, winged and all other peoples inside the Sacred Circle that surrounds Him.'

Dawn Boy watched while the fire-sticks were piled to the four directions and a teepee shape of sticks was formed over them to represent the dome of the sky; then four rocks were placed upon the pile to indicate the four directions, and other rocks piled on top of them so that when the fire burned it would heat them red hot. After appropriate prayers and the lighting of the fire all who were to be purified watched the leader, Sees-beyond-the-Lightning enter the lodge, while a woman stayed outside to act as helper. A hole was dug in the center of the floor of the lodge to represent Wankan-Tanka, and a prayer said asking for the purification of all within, then a deeper pit was dug for the hot stones and the dirt sprinkled in a line toward the east, ending in a small mound in front of the fire. Then the holy man began the prayer:

"Upon You Mother Earth we build the sacred path, the good red road, and on this path we walk firmly, purifying ourselves that we may follow this path even to Wakan Tanka. May we be pure. May we have new life!

"Grandfather! Grandfather! You Wakan-Tanka have taught us the four sacred steps and now we shall step them with good hearts. Through all living things we send our songs to you and ask for your mercy and help. Help us to follow the Sacred Way that our people may live!"

Dawn Boy felt his blood tingling as he entered the lodge with the others and took his place with his back close to the willow framework, and as he entered he prayed:

"Thank you, Wakan-Tanka. By bending my body low to enter this lodge I show how small I am compared to You, who are everything. Purify me so I may send my cry to You from the mountain and be answered. Help us all to be purified today, so that we may do your Will!"

Inside more prayers were said, and tobacco powder thrown to the four directions and up to Father Sky and down to Mother Earth. Then the whole lodge was purified by the leader burning sweet grass with a hot coal and wafting the sacred smoke over everybody and everything.

Dawn Boy saw the Sacred Pipe passed into the lodge by the helper, first to the man who was sitting at the west. This man placed it before him with the stem pointing to the west. Then, with his nerves tingling, Dawn Boy watched the first of the red hot rocks passed into the lodge by the helper. It was placed in the very center of the lodge in the middle of the pit where it represented Wakan Tanka Himself. Next came rocks for the west, the north, the east and the south, followed by many more till the hole was filled with them and the heat became stronger and stronger. As each rock came it was touched by the stem of the Sacred Pipe, and all gave a loud cry of welcome.

Now the Sacred Pipe was smoked by the west man to the four directions and up to the sky and down to the earth, and then passed sun-wise around the circle, each taking a puff.

Dawn Boy watched as the pipe was passed back to and emptied by the west man, and then passed to Sees-beyond-the Lightning, who sat at the east. The holy man swung it around the Sacred Circle above the hot stones, then handed it to the helper outside the door to be refilled with tobacco and placed on the Sacred Earth Mound by the fire, with its stem pointing westward, the first of the directions to be prayed to.

The door of the lodge was then closed and all present were plunged into darkness, which represented the darkness of the spirit and all bad thoughts and deeds from which all were to be purified during the four parts of the ceremony, for the darkness would come four times and the light come back four times each time the door was opened, symbolizing the four ages of the earth.

Four times and each time to one of the directions, a man's voice sang a prayer calling for the purification of all in the lodge and the opening of their souls and minds so the light of Wankan Tanka would come. And four times water was poured on the hot rocks till the steam rose so thick and the lodge became so hot that all had to bow their noses almost to the floor in order to breathe.

As Dawn Boy heard the voices singing the sacred prayer songs and felt the sweat pour from his bent body, he also sang inwardly to the Great Spirit, asking to be purified that he might help his people and be one with the universe and all good things. He knew that the sweat pouring from his body symbolized the impurities of life being drawn from him, and he felt so lifted by the songs, like an eagle rising on the winds towards the sun, that his heart seemed to turn over and over and he knew, as one knows his own breath, that the wisdom and goodness of the Great Spirit would guide him.

During the time of the sweat-bath, every once in a while a little boy or girl would stick a head under the flap, and cry in a thin frightened voice: "Oh Wakan-Tanka, give me strength and goodness, too!"

And always Sees-beyond-the Lightning would say in his wise old voice:

"The child is pure from the beginning, but it is the purity of weakness; now must we turn back to this same purity, but make it the purity of a man, make it the purity of strength!"

Finally the time came after more than an hour of intense sweating for the door to be opened for the last time, and all present cried: "Hi ho! Thank you Wakan Tanka!" thanking Him for the coming of the light of the spirit that was now filling the souls of those present. Then the helper brought a hot coal to Sees-beyond-the-Lightning and he burned some sweet grass with it, singing: "Smell the sweet fragrance of Wankan Tanka. Through it we will be purified and be happy. But this Sacred Fire must be used in a sacred manner, or it can harm us greatly. Be careful, be careful! Every moment of your life!"

With a last prayer to the Great Spirit, the leader passed his hands through the sacred smoke and, moving sunwise, all those from the lodge passed out into the glowing light, their faces radiant with joy, their bodies streaming with sweat. And Dawn Boy came forth into the sunlight tingling all over and feeling ready in his heart for the great ordeal on the mountain, the search for a vision that would shape his life.

chapter TWELVE

The Sacred Pipe – Guide to a Vision and to Life

SONG OF THE SKY LOOM

"O our Mother the Earth, O our Father the Sky
Your children are we, and with tired backs
We bring you the gifts that you love.
Then weave for us a garment of brightness;
May the warp be the white light of morning,
May the weft be the red light of evening,
May the fringes be the falling rain,
May the border be the standing rainbow.
Thus weave for us a garment of brightness,
That we may walk fittingly where birds sing,
That we may walk fittingly where grass is green,
O our Mother the Earth, O our Father the Sky!"

Song from the Tewa Pueblos, translated by Dr. Herbert T. Spinden, p. 76 of *The Sky Clears*—Poetry of the American Indians, by A. Grove Day, Univ. of Nebraska Press, 1951.

THE ABOVE SONG EXEMPLIFIES THE feeling of the Native American for the sacred beauty of earth and sky, and how he himself must become a part of that by living a beautiful life. Symbolically the Sacred Pipe expresses the same feeling whenever the Indian holds it up during a ceremony or vision search; in fact, at all times it is a magic symbol of the power of the Spirit. Thus the white man who looks on this pipe as only something to smoke misses completely its whole meaning and is as blind to its spirit as the totally blind man is to the sunlight.

How does what starts out as a plain piece of hollowed wood and hollow stone attain this sacred meaning and power? It attains them entirely through what those who touch, shape it, decorate it, and hold it put into it. Especially the owner of the pipe must visualize in it, with clarity and power, its reflection of earth and sky, mineral, plant life, animal and bird life, human life, and the Great Spirit, Himself.

Look at a large and hard rock and visualize the strength in it, the hardness of it, and its everlasting nature, for it has probably been much as it is now for millions of years. How petty then is the shortness of our lives compared to that great time; yet we can partake of that age and durability if we make our hearts one with the universe and purge away all the petty desires and vices that limit our vision.

The rock or stone from which the pipe bowl is made is always very special. Thus the red smooth sandstone from which my pipe's bowl is made comes from the sacred pipestone quarry in Minnesota where, for generations without number, the Native Americans of both woodlands and prairie have come in peace to gather stones for the sacred pipes. Even mortal enemies came together on these sacred grounds of the calumet (red pipe) rocks and touched hands in friendship. It is a rock blessed by the Great Spirit with special beauty and special ease of carving, yet it is durable enough to last for many centuries. The circle of the bowl of the pipe becomes to the user the Circle of the Universe, the Circle of Earth and its Life, and the Circle of Mankind. Look on it then with great reverence for this meaning.

Look at a tree and see within it the everlasting fire, something that makes it far greater in meaning than just the visual image. Thus it started as a seed that was nurtured by the sun and grew into a sapling, and that sun's fire became part of its inner being as the tree grew into a sapling, then finally produced flowers and fruits, and always the wood that, in time of need, can bring through fire the breath and spirit of the sun to man.

The stem of the pipe is usually made of cottonwood, not only because this wood is easy to bore, but, more importantly, because it is a wood that echoes the voice of the waters which are always near where this tree grows and where the Voice of the Great Spirit is heard when the wind whispers and murmurs in its leaves. The clear channel of the hole in the stem symbolizes the open hearts and minds we must have to let the Spirit truly reach us. Think of these things when you look at the stem and understand that every part of this pipe is singing a song of the Spirit and its many manifestations. If one cannot grasp this, then the pipe is only stone and wood, but that one has lost something of more value to his life than a room full of gold and diamonds! There are great lessons here as to how to make our lives harmonious with the rhythm of the universe.

Usually attached to the pipe in some way are the skin or teeth or bone of an animal and the feathers of a bird, particularly among the Plains tribes something from a buffalo, and the feathers of the eagle. To them the buffalo is the great symbol of the gift from the Great Spirit of food, and also of all animal life. The eagle feathers, of course, are most sacred because they come from a bird who, above all others, flies and soars into the sky until it disappears, teaching human beings to fly in the same way with their spirits up and up into the everlasting sky of the Grandfather, the Lord of Being. And in the feel of these feathers and the skin of the animal we draw strength and wisdom from other life than that of human-kind; we find kinship with them and can use their powers if we are wise. In fact many a vision is of bird or animal, and the vision seeker is taught through them by the Master of Life, how to live and make his life great in spirit ways.

All these powers and blessings and knowledge come to us through faith, for if we cannot believe, then the pipe becomes only a stick with a piece of stone attached, hence nothing but a curiosity, powerless to aid us who give nothing in return.

As my knowledge and friendship with Indians increased I became vaguely aware of the power some of the old ones had, and I remembered more vividly the early dawn when I had watched Chio Jari, the Guaymi Indian youth, singing his dawn song and sensed the Spirit pouring from him like a living thing. That they had something in their lives of far greater value than anything I had was symbolized to me by the sacred pipe, and I desired to have one of my own. So one day up in the plains country of southern South Dakota near White River I met a Sundance Chief of the Hunkapapa Sioux who had a newly-made pipe with a beautiful red sandstone bowl from the sacred quarry in Minnesota, and it had a white cottonwood stem, all as yet undecorated and uncarved. I asked him what he wanted for it, telling him I had long wanted to have a sacred pipe and make it sacred in my life. He named a price that was well beyond what I could afford at that time, but he took pity on me when he saw how my face had fallen in despair, and parted with it at a much lower figure. Then he looked at me sternly, and said:

"I have given you this pipe for far less than it is worth, so it is partly a gift, and I want you to use this gift in a holy manner. The pipe has just been made, so it is dead at present, and it will stay dead until you have a vision about it. Pray for this vision and keep a pure heart so that you will be worthy of the pipe when the vision comes. The vision will show you how to decorate the pipe, so do nothing with it until that time."

I am sure if he had not seen at least some sincerity in what I had said about the pipe, he would never have given me the pipe under any circumstances at such a price nor told me what he did. The pipe I would probably have taken home and decorated in a way I thought appropriate, but it would have forever remained a dead pipe and little more than a curiosity which I could show to friends. Having at least the beginning of faith made the difference and so I became acquainted with my pipe in a sacred way.

For years I waited and prayed, but no vision came and I began to despair that it ever would. Frankly, though, I am somewhat mystified that a vision came at all, because I never felt I reached the full state of purification that was required, but perhaps the Great Spirit took pity on me.

So one night three years after I received the pipe I had a beautiful dream in which I saw my pipe floating in the air with an aura of light about it. Slowly the stem became carved in a meaningful way, the colors formed on the different parts, a rawhide cord became attached to a group of eagle feathers, and I saw a little ball of something made of skin. Also in the dream I seemed to know what almost everything meant.

The pipe bowl, of course, meant the unity and harmony of all living things with the Great Spirit, including mankind's eventual coming into the circle of harmony (see accompanying illustration). The reddish-brown stone bowl meant the red-brown skin of Mother Earth and the durability and lasting quality of rock which we must strive to learn by being faithful and strong in character. The stem above was decorated with long green triangles symbolic of plant life and of growth in the spirit. The yellow areas symbolized the golden light of the sun and the Holy

Spirit that comes to us from the Sky Father. The red crosses indicated the four directions, each with its powers, courage from the west, strength from the north, wisdom from the east and spiritual growth from the south, plus the good red road of life—a pathway in which honesty and purity dominate every thought. The blue patches on the stem indicated Father Sky Himself, the Great Giver and Knower, to whose will we must all bend as the tree bows before the wind. The brown on the underside of the stem could only mean the humble spirit of Mother Earth, who lets us walk on her to show how to be humble, yet produces all the good things that make life possible.

The four eagle feathers hanging from the pipe indicate the four direc-

tions again with all their powers, but also are symbolic of the spiritual power of the eagle who climbs towards the sun, and whose flight we must follow in the Spirit if we are to join with the Sky Father and make our lives beautiful. I was not given to understand the ball of skin until much later, as it took a while to grasp its meaning and just what I should use for it. Fools Crow, a Medicine Man of the Oglala Sioux, blessed my pipe with the sacred incense of burning sweet grass and gave me a small ball of hide from a calf buffalo, which he told me represented the spirit of all animal life, even as the eagle feathers represented all the birds and their spirit. This ball was tied to the pipe at the junction of stem and bowl. No animal was held more sacred than the buffalo, with the possible exception of the otter, so that this buffalo skin represented all the high animal powers.

I have a doeskin Sacred Pipe Bag (see illustration), which Fools Crow and others of the Oglala Sioux identified in 1967 as having once belonged to Crazy Horse, the great Sioux warrior and holy man. This bag had been given my father, a doctor, in 1895 on the Pine Ridge Reservation in South Dakota for saving a chief's son's life. My father had refused pay for his work because he saw how bad the conditions of the Sioux were in those days, but the chief insisted he keep the bag because the chief had been given a vision about the bag in which he was told to give it to the first white man who helped his family without pay. This giving, he was told, would one day bring much good to the Indian peoples.

I keep the bag and the Sacred Pipe in the same place, as I feel they both have great power, but my pipe is kept in a pair of red cloth bags as the Sioux pipe bag is too old and fragile to be used anymore as a carrier. This is the same pipe that I used in 1967 during my vision search on the top of Bear Butte, the sacred mountain of the Plains tribes (see Chapter Nineteen).

The power of the pipe and the bag are built on faith. They are not fetishes to be worshiped, as the missionaries to the Indians often believed, but are purely symbolic aids in making me remember to daily seek the power of the Spirit and to purify my heart. I know I have many times failed in this, but I know also that all life is a great struggle, in which we go both up and down, but these symbols—like the cross to the ardent Christian—help keep me mainly on the upward trail. And who has the right to judge others save the Lord of us All??

chapter THIRTEEN

The Youth Searches for a Vision

DREAM SONG

"At night may I roam,
Against the winds may I roam,
At night may I roam,
When the owl is hooting may I roam.

At dawn may I roam,
Against the winds may I roam,
At dawn may I roam,
When the crow is calling may I roam."

Sioux personal medicine song, from *The Sky Clears*, p. 100, by A. Grove Day. University of Nebraska Press, 1951.

WHEN DAWN BOY CAME TO find Sees-beyond-the-Lightning to start on his vision quest, he wore only his breech clout and his moccasins. He had finished the Inipi, the purification ceremony in the sweat lodge, and was now ready for the Hanblecheyapi, the going to the mountain top to seek a vision. He was carrying his filled pipe with him and, when he entered the lodge of the old man, he pointed the stem towards his teacher and sat down. When seated, he turned the pipe around so the stem of the pipe pointed towards himself.

Sees-beyond-the Lightning took the pipe in his wrinkled brown hands and raised it towards the sky, Wakan-Tanka.

"What do you wish?" he asked.

"I wish to send my voice to the Powers Above, and I need your help."

"How! This is good!" He beckoned with his hand and Dawn Boy followed him out of the teepee to a knoll where Sees-beyond-the-Lightning lifted the stem of the pipe again to the sky.

"Hay-ay-hay-eee-eee" he cried four times, "Oh Grandfather, Wakan-Tanka; You who started the world; to You belongs all that is and will ever be! Purify this youth so he may send his voice and offer his pipe to You. To the high place he will go seeking You and he will walk in sacredness and beauty. Help him! That he and his children to come will live in purity and goodness."

Now the old man turned to the young man and said: "It is useless for you to go on this quest unless you are willing to turn your whole soul to the search. In the bad times we know are coming to our people many will turn away from this search and forget and be lost. Therefore, I am asking you today not to seek powers just for yourself, but to seek them mainly that they may help your people. You must so purify yourself that generations to come will feel the power, and in the darkest days that lie ahead at least one among your children's children or their children will say to himself or herself, "my grandfather or great-grandfather knew the Sacred Way, and I also will seek it and follow it!"

"When you are on the mountain and even when you are climbing up to it, listen to the voices that sing with the wind among the leaves; watch the trees and birds and animals and even the insects with all your heart and mind and see within them the powers of Wakan-Tanka, so you will be ever alert when voices speak to you or a vision comes. It may come in only a small way, as with a tiny ant crawling on a stick, but you will see and hear nothing if you do not watch and listen with the eyes and ears of the fox! All about you is the great mystery of the universe, of this earth, of every living thing, and among them is much sacredness and wisdom that is hidden from men, except those who seek with a pure and open heart, dedicated to their people. Now go and be wise and let every thought be guided by the Spirit!"

Dawn Boy was given two helpers to go with him and prepare the place of his vision search, but he also carried with him a bag of the sacred tobacco, five straight sticks of the wild red cherry, and his sacred pipe. The helpers had gathered a large quantity of the leafy outerparts of sagebrush, which they stuffed into two bags and carried with them.

The three rode their horses far across the plain until they came to the foot of a high and lonely hill.

"Here many famous warriors have sought their visions," said one of the helpers. He handed to Dawn Boy a large buffalo robe which he would use for protection when sleeping on the sagebrush at the top of the peak. As Dawn Boy began to climb the hill's steep slope, he pointed his pipe stem forward. The two helpers moved ahead of him with the bags of sagebrush and the five cherry sticks, while he came more slowly, praying and calling to the spirits of hill and life as he moved upward, asking that they might receive him.

"I come," he called, "with love for you, you hill, and all you trees and shrubs, even the little grasses and flowers, for you are all children of the Above One. All you animals and birds listen to me also, for I come with love for you and all living things, for we are all part of one circle. You I have not come to harm, but to seek your help and that of Wakan-Tanka, not for myself, but for my people, that they may live! And you, Mother Earth, be good to me when I rest upon you, for from you come many blessings and you help all things to live; help me then to live in purity and wisdom, in courage and strength, that I may help many people."

As he walked along, now and then praying and singing, he was also very attentive to everything he saw or heard. Each rock he passed he saw had a special character, some brown, some red, some green, some covered with lichens and moss, others smooth, but all with that great feeling of strength the rock people have. There was a warm breeze blowing so each tree was singing to him with its leaves, and he listened as if he could understand words they were saying, and indeed he felt they were echoing back the love and purity he was building in his own mind, for deep inside he knew the absolute vital necessity to make his thoughts like the clear waters of the little creek that tossed down the hillside from the heights above, or like the pure blue of the sky. And so it seemed the wind and leaves were saying to him:

"Dawn Boy! Dawn Boy! Have no fear, little brother, for we will help you. Sing with us when you reach the top of the high hill and we will help your songs waft to the sky. Make your heart open like the stem of your Sacred Pipe and we will carry into it the answers of the Silent One."

Now the bright-colored butterflies were dancing around him as he strode slowly up the hill, and one even lit on his pipestem, folding its wings up and down as if to say:

"We too bring you blessings, Dawn Boy. Keep your heart strong and we will help you." So he looked on the butterflies with great love, and watched them fly before him with joy.

All about him birds were singing, for it was the highest season of the sun when the birds nest. He heard the rasping calls of kingbirds, and the *pippety-chee* of the phoebe, the whistled *"tsick-dee-de-deeteee"* song of a Black-capped Chickadee from a nearby juniper, and the long, thrilling, trilling "cheeee-pooo cheeee-poooo!" of the Rock Wren. And all their cries and songs seemed to be saying:

"Courage, little brother; have no fear even in the darkness and the storm, for the Great Spirit speaks to you through us, and He will be with you."

On the rocks the ground squirrels were playing and they seemed almost in song as they whistled at one another. As he went higher, he noticed that they seemed to become less and less afraid of him, as if they too felt his love for them. And he sensed they were saying:

"Because your heart is good, Dawn Boy, and you do not come to harm us, we also will bless you."

When he reached the top of the high hill, he found the two helpers had prepared his bed of the sacred sagebrush so that its sweet aroma rose all about him as he approached, and they also had placed the five cherry sticks upright in the ground, one at the very center of the highest spot on the hills, and the others all about four yards away from the center to the four directions. Then silently they left him, for there was nothing more to do nor to be said until he came down from his long vigil.

Soon he laid his buffalo-hide blanket down on the sagebrush so that when he slept his head would be toward the center spot, which represented symbolically the center of the universe. Then he took his sacred tobacco and sprinkled it in a complete circle all around where he would be crying for a vision. Next he took off his loin cloth and his moccasins that he might be untouched save by wind and sun before the Lord of the Skies. Last he took his Sacred Pipe and, with the stem pointed out, began a slow stepping in and out to each of the cardinal directions from the center, and a still slower circling from left to right, sunwise, around the Sacred Circle.

At each farthest out place near a stick that marked a direction, he would stand for a while praying to the powers of that direction, first to west, then to north, then to east and last to south before starting over. To the west he prayed for courage, to the north for strength, to the east for wisdom and to the south for growth. Then he would point the pipe straight up to the sky and call to the Spirit who is Lord of us all. Then down to Mother Earth he pointed the pipe that he might partake of her humbleness and goodness, and back again to Father Sky that he might draw the Spirit down into his own heart. And so did he cover the seven Sacred Directions. Each time he paused he also chanted the ancient Sioux song: "Wakan-Tanka onshimala ye oyate wani wachin cha!" ("Oh Great Spirit, be merciful to me that my people may live!")

Soon a rhythm was started that was like the great heartbeat of the earth itself, or like the beat of vast waters crashing on a beach. And always his mind remained concentrated on the spirit, hour after hour, knowing this had to grow stronger and stronger if he was to be worthy of help from the Great Spirit. And hour after hour also he prayed to grow in purity of his own heart so that he would be too strong for temptations to pull him down from his high duty to his people and to Wankan-Tanka.

When the darkness crept over the earth and up the hillside like a great dark curtain and the quavering whistle of a screech owl wafted up the slope, he lay down to rest on his bed of sagebrush and under his buffalo robe, thankful for its warmth as a protection against the cold. Here he slept for some hours, but woke in the middle of the night, as he knew he must, to sing his songs to the cold stars in the black sky, his robe wrapped tightly about him, but his pipe pointing to the directions one by one, then up to Father Sky and down to Mother Earth.

Again he slept but woke up an hour before the dawn, knowing as well as if he had an alarm clock when that moment came, and that he must face the Morning Star and ask it to carry a Message from him to the Great Spirit. And as he woke, he suddenly tensed, for he sensed something large and fierce near him in the darkness, and almost he gave way to fear and would have lain there shaking and trembling. But he remembered that Sees-beyond-the-Lightning had warned him that great beasts might come and even strange evil powers, but he would be safe as long as he kept his thoughts on the Spirit. For a while he heard a deep rasping breathing, but silently he prayed for strength and at last he heard heavy footsteps fading away down the hill.

So he rose up and stood wrapped in his robe, but with a naked arm extending his pipe to the east so the stem pointed to the bright orb of the Morning Star, and he sang:

"Oh Son of the Morning, Messenger of the Great Spirit, give me your blessing and take my cry to Him who is Above us All, and is before us and beyond us forever. Tell Him I am crying for a vision and for spirit power that I may help my people. Tell Him that I am less than the dust beneath my feet, but I ask Him for help that my people may live. You who are the brightest of the Winged Ones of Heaven take Him my message!"

Slowly the light grew out of a grayness in the east, the sun's rays burst upon the green emerald waves of the grassy Great Plains, and the youth brought his prayer songs to crescendo, for he knew this was the most sacred moment of the whole day. This was the moment when the rising sun symbolized the way the Great Spirit comes to all people at special times to wake them from the darkness of selfishness and evil and bring them into the light of His love, and teach them the way of honor and of obedience to His will.

So filled with ecstacy and spirit was the youth that the whole day passed like a glorious song in which he felt neither hunger nor thirst, for he was drinking from the imperishable waters of the Spirit that are given only to the true seekers after the glory of the Above One. He saw the ants climb in their lines to the tops of the grass stalks to gather the drying seeds. He watched the swallows zoom over the hilltop like flying bullets, and the eagle rise from the earth below till he was only a dot that finally disappeared into the very center of the blue, and Dawn Boy's spirit rose also to soar towards the Sun and to the Lord of Being, and always he sang the simple beautiful songs that were his offering and his soul.

Night came again and a third day, but it was late in the afternoon of this third day that a crisis rose to test his spirit. Great dark clouds began to gather in the west and move towards him and he saw far off the flashing of lightning. He knew the Thunder Beings were talking in the rumbling distant boom that came to him and the Thunder Birds were beginning to hurl the lightning down to Mother Earth along with the pouring rain that brings life to the land. But he knew also that the lightning would be most likely to strike on this high hilltop and he soon would be in great danger. So he lifted his prayers in even greater strength than before, increasing their earnestness and powers as the dark clouds shut out the light of the sun and the thunder boomed closer and closer.

He relaxed his body and mind now by a supreme act of the will, so he did not tense when the first drops of rain fell or when the lightning suddenly blazed close by in a violent strike at the hilltop. Thunder almost instantly smashed against his eardrums in a tearing sound like the massed roaring of a hundred monsters, and he wavered for a second like a tall tree in a storm. But still his voice came strong from his throat:

"I am at the center of the universe, calling to the Great Spirit to help my people, to give me power to help them; today is a good day to die!" And his voice came so firmly that even when another terrible crashing roar sounded behind him after a flash of light that all but blinded him, he still stood poised on the hilltop singing and his heart was strong.

Then the rain fell in driving sheets but somehow, though it was all about him, it was not within the Sacred Circle he had made with the tobacco and his heart swelled with knowledge that the Powers were protecting him. The storm moved on from the hilltop, growling, muttering and flashing, but the sounds slowly lessened and, in the late afternoon the sunlight burst through the clouds in shafts of glory. In an hour the sun was setting through drifting clouds upon which the sunlight's gold, red and purple played like music, painting itself in beauty, and he prayed to that beauty and its Maker with all his heart and soul.

When darkness came he lay down thankfully on his bed of sagebrush, again wrapped in his buffalo robe and falling calmly into a deep sleep. After a time he sensed his eyes opening, for there was about him an eerie greenish light that outlined the few little pines crowning the hilltop in a ghostly glow, and he thought he heard a deep voice talking until he realized it was the "hoo-hoo-hoo-hooo!" of a Great Horned Owl.

Generations of his people had told their children that the owl people were often the messengers of dark spirits and sometimes stole little ones from their mothers away into the darkness, but somehow his spirit was so strong from his experience with the recent lightning and thunder that he had no fear. Instead, he watched carefully and soon saw an owl perched on a branch of one of the trees. It turned its head to look at him and the first faint glow of starlight in its eyes increased in intensity until the eyes were two large circles of light. Then he knew that he was in the midst of a vision and that the owl was no ordinary owl of the dark night, but a spirit owl with power, maybe the grandfather of all the owls. So he spoke without trembling:

"Even as a child I liked to hear the voices of the owl people! Why have you come grandfather?"

And the deep voice came back like an echo out of the stillness and the night's mystery, so he was not sure whether it was really the owl or his own heartbeat that was answering.

"Listen, Dawn Boy! Listen! There is a darkness coming to your people, and in the darkness is when evil is done. I have come to give you the power to see in the darkness and hear in it and understand what you are seeing and hearing. I will also help you to be able to run in the dark and never stumble. You will heal those whom evil coming in the night has made sick, and you will help those who are in danger and who will listen, but let those who will not listen go their way, for they are lost in their own foolishness."

"And how shall I know the wisdom to give them?"

"I am only a power sent by the Great Spirit; you will pray to Him through me and wisdom will come. Carry an owl's feather in your hair, carry one hanging from your Sacred Pipe; put one in your medicine bag, and this will remind you that I am near. Always when darkness comes, I will be flying above you and around you, but have no fear. I shall be there to help you and your people."

Then all the lights faded away and Dawn Boy dropped into deeper sleep again, but happily, knowing a vision had come.

Now he seemed to wake in the dawn, yet somehow it was not the real dawn for the light that hung over the hilltop seemed to be coming from everywhere and not like that of the sun, and he was startled by the knowledge that he was having a second vision, for a crow was perched on the same branch where the owl had been before and it, too, was talking to him.

"Dawn Boy! Dawn Boy!" it exclaimed. "I am your helper in the daylight, even as the owl is your helper when night comes. Day and night form the balance in the life of a man, and so do you need powers also of the daytime during the bad times coming. Evil will stalk the land and evil will strike your people, but you must be too strong to be harmed by it. We crow people are noted for our wisdom and the ways we can trick men. Watch us carefully in the months and years ahead and you will see some of our tricks which we will teach you. We know when men are about to shoot at us and we know how to dodge. We know where good hiding places are and how to use them so none can find us. With our powers and those of the owl, you will escape danger and live a long time; you will be wise in the ways of your enemies and help your people against them. You will need all these powers badly, so watch and study very carefully. When you are very old we will bring you one of your great grandchildren who will listen and to him you will pass on your sacred knowledge that we give you from Wakan-Tanka. But let those who will not listen go their way, for they are a lost people!"

When Dawn Boy woke up at the fourth dawn, he knew he had the powers he needed for there beside his bed of sagebrush lay one owl feather and a single feather of a crow. Reverently he gathered them up and put them in his hair, binding them so they would hold, and knowing they were magic feathers. Then he put his buffalo robe up on the central black cherry pole as a signal and waited while he sent out his prayers to the rising sun.

At noon the helpers came and assisted him down the hillside, for he was very weak after nearly four days and four nights of fasting without food and water, but his spirit was very strong. When he was led into the sweat lodge several hours later, he seated himself on the west, with the stem of his sacred pipe pointing toward the east. Soon Sees-beyond-the Lightning entered also, passed around behind him, then came back to the east where he seated himself. Others followed and took their places, all old men with solemn faces and searching eyes. The five sacred rocks were brought in, each hot from the fire and placed in the proper directions, then other hot rocks of the number required. In the glowing heat, the old wise one spoke:

"How! It is well that we are here together to hear your story. You have sent your words by way of your pipe to Wakan-Tanka, to the powers of the four directions, down to Mother Earth, and inward to your heart, asking for power to help your people. All these have seen you and your pipe, and all else that is sacred in the universe. If you were always sincere in your calling on the mountain, then you have made this pipe sacred, too. You must now tell us the truth, and be very careful that you make up no story, for Wankan-Tanka is listening also. Your pipe also is sacred and it too will listen. If you lie at all, the Powers of the Universe will punish you!"

Sees-beyond-the-Lightning now arose and walked around the lodge in a sun-wise direction once, and then seated himself to the right of Dawn Boy. On a pile of buffalo chips placed in front of the young man he placed the pipe with its stem pointing to the sky. Removing the tallow seal from the bowl of the pipe, he lit the tobacco with a hot coal, offered the pipe to the Seven Directions, and then touched the stem to the mouth of Dawn Boy. Circling the stem in the air once more, the old man smoked for a few moments, then again touched the lips of the young man. The smoking was continued until all who were in the sacred circle of the lodge had each puffed it. After this it was emptied of its ashes and purified in the incense of burning sweet grass.

For the last time Sees-beyond-the-Lightning lifted the pipe and pointed its stem at Dawn Boy, saying: "For four days and four nights we have been praying for you and praying that the pipe would become sacred and lead you to the powers. Speak now and tell us what you saw and heard."

Dawn Boy bowed his head in humbleness, then straightened up and looked straight into the eyes of the old man as he told his story. He omitted no detail, but when he reached the time of the lightning striking near him, he felt that everybody was listening intently. When he told the story of the owl, he saw they were breathing deeply, but when he repeated the words the crow had given him he saw their eyes were wide in amazement.

When the account of the two visions was finished, there was silence for a long time, while all watched him closely. He knew that all of these old men were very wise in detecting signs of a false story, but he sat confidently and calmly waiting.

At last Sees-beyond-the-Lightning stretched forward his hand reverently and touched the young man's knee lightly.

"Washtai! Washtai Wakan! (this is very good and holy). You have been very fortunate. You have had two great visions and been given wonderful powers to help your people." As he paused there was a long sighing in the silence, and all the other men present let out their breaths in a long hiss of approval.

"But remember," continued the old wise one, "that you must constantly strengthen these powers and your humbleness and purity by daily being alert to watch and learn from everything you can observe about you, and by sending prayers and silent thankfulness to the Above One. For you can lose all that you have gained very quickly if you let your desires overcome you or become filled with pride. Whenever you feel yourself weakening go soon alone to a hilltop again and send your voices out with the Sacred Pipe to Wakan-Tanka. Seek more strength then for your visions or even new visions, and if your heart is good and sincere as it has been on this vision search, the Great Ones will help you."

Then he prayed:

"Oh Wakan-Tanka. You have brought great bounty to this young man and given him two strong helpers who will always be with him as long as he is sincere and his heart is pure and humble. Make him strong and careful every day that his heart and mind shall dwell in the high places and see with Your eyes. Then shall he bring great value to his people and help them through the bad days. Be kind to all of us, oh Great Spirit, that we may follow you with good hearts and minds to the end!"

And all present lifted their hands and sang a sacred chant:

"Grandfather, behold me! Grandfather, behold me!

I held my pipe and offered it to You, that my people may live!"

chapter FOURTEEN

The Broken Pipe

"Father have pity on me,
Father have pity on me;
I am crying for thirst,
I am crying for thirst;
All is gone—I have nothing to eat,
All is gone—I have nothing to eat."

An Arapaho Ghost Dance Song, from page 977 of *The Ghost Dance Religion*, by James Mooney, 14th Annual Report of the Bureau of Ethnology, 1892-93.

THIS PATHETIC SONG IS ACTUALLY a calling more for spiritual drink and food than for the material, though the Indians of the time had indeed lost the major source of their food, killed off by the whites, the buffaloes. But it also expresses the despair of the Indian as all that was beautiful in his past was pulled down and hidden by the curtain of white civilization. The old songs no longer seemed to have power, the vision seekers no longer seemed to find visions, and the very earth itself seemed to be turning ugly under the profaning hands of the profit-makers and polluters. As one old Indian told me once, "Our teepee is turned upside down."

Before, most of the people had been close to the spirit, praying and singing in the dawn, at noon, at sunset and to the diamond-sprinkled sky of night. Always they had felt surrounded by the powers of the Above One, so that every act must be done in a sacred manner. Most white people made no effort to understand this. Instead, most of them laughed at or ridiculed almost everything the Native American did, saying most of it was superstitious, or some kind of savagery, urging the natives to follow the white man's way and go to the white man's church. But those who knew the old way and did go to the churches too often found that white people made a form and a showing out of their religion without having the depth of feeling to really live it. For the Indian children, however, often the white laughter and scorn struck home and something beautiful was killed within them. Many turned against their parents, or were brainwashed when taken away to school, and they began to agree with their new masters, saying to themselves, the only hope is to be like them.

Many a sacred pipe was put away and hidden in the days when the Native American felt himself slipping down into darkness of the spirit. Indeed, symbolically the pipe had become broken, for its spiritual meaning was becoming lost and when lost it became only a piece of wood and stone. A still greater loss was that the Sacred Tree, which symbolized the spiritual tree that gave life and unity to the tribe, was dying. Thus, the Aztec grieved after his people had been conquered:

"I foresaw, being a Mexican, that our rule began to be destroyed;
I went forth weeping that it was to bow down and be destroyed."
(From *Ancient Nahuatl Poetry,* Library of American Aboriginal Literature,
Vol. 7, 1887.)

The change that came over the Indian is told very poignantly in a book
called *An Autobiography of a Winnebago,* by Paul Radin. In this story
the man tells how he was raised at a time around the close of the
nineteenth century when the old values were breaking down as the
young men and women were listening to the siren songs of the white
people about how they must become civilized. Thus the young man of
the story is pulled both ways, both towards his old people and towards
the white people. Still, when his father asks him to go to a high hill to
seek a vision, he agrees to do so. On the top of the hill, however, his
mind is not committed to the job of finding a vision because of the many
doubtful thoughts the white people have put into him.

Unable to concentrate his mind on the spirit search, he thinks of
women and gambling and other things he would rather do than be up
there alone on the hilltop truly seeking a vision. Consequently he has no
vision, but the importance of finding a vision has been drummed into him
since childhood and he realizes having a vision will give him prestige and
power with his people. In the old days no youth would have, in most
cases, considered for a moment making up a vision and telling a lie
because he would have felt the Spirit would punish him severely. But
this young man, through associations with poorer class whites, had
given in before to the easy way of getting what he wanted by telling lies,
and so he decides to tell one now. He does not realize that just by making
this decision he has killed something fine within himself, something of
far more value than anything the lie might get him.

Half-stupefied with his own ego and the foolish idea that he can bluff
people into believing him, he comes before a group of old men in the
sweat lodge and tells of a beautiful vision he has had, a vision which
exists only in his own imagination. Then he looks up into their eyes,
those dark and wise old eyes, and sees that not one has believed him;
everyone knows he has lied. They do not say anything, but they do not
need to. Something dies inside him. He leaves the sweat lodge like a
whipped cur and from then on he follows what some Indians call the
"black road." It is a road that spirals downward, ever downward,
through more lies, through the whisky bottle and the drunkenness it
brings, and through fights since he is still strong enough to beat up other
men, and for a while, this gives him temporary satisfaction. Also he
takes up with many loose women who are following the same road,
gambles away his money, steals when he can get away with it, but finds

himself in and out of jails, and going down and down into darkness until he wakes one day with the whole story of his life before him like a painted nightmare and the stark knowledge that there is no hope unless he finds a way back to the Great Spirit. In trying to go back he finds the Peyote people of the Native American Church, and a way at last to find visions with the help of Peyote and thus some help to get out of his failure. It is a useful crutch, but he still has a long journey ahead before coming back to anything equal to what he lost.

All over America there is the same story of the downfall of peoples once highly motivated by their surroundings, attuned with earth and sky, and many of them highly moral. Thus Catlin, the famous artist who lived eight years among the Plains tribes in the old days, wrote: "They payed the strictest regard to decency and cleanliness and elegance of dress." He also said: "No Indian ever betrayed me, struck me a blow, or stole from me a shilling's worth of property that I am aware of."

Long ago one missionary, deep in Indian country, was leaving his cabin for several months and was worried about its contents, but his Indian guide told him: "Have no fear. There is not a white man within a hundred miles!" Such was the Indian record before too much white contact.

But all this changed with the coming of what we call civilization. Still we must resist the temptation to blame white people for all this. Of course there were always some bad ones, but the majority of the white people were, on the whole, honorably disposed and certainly the missionaries had good intentions. But the main trouble lay in other directions. One was complete lack of understanding of Native Americans by most whites and the dogmatic attitude that, since theirs was a superior culture and religion, as they thought, they therefore had the right to force both on the Indians. Combined with these, of course, were their overwhelming numbers, their technical ability to wage war more terribly and with better organization, and their hunger for land and gold.

Actually, Native American culture and religion were both beautiful and deeply meaningful to the Indians. To take this away from them as was often done brutally and without understanding, produced a shocking effect on a sensitive and wonderful people. The Sacred Pipe was indeed broken by culture shock, a shock so great that thousands literally died of broken hearts, and myriad others took the dark road of alcohol with its rosy but only temporary dream of a better world. So large numbers of many tribes became a broken people, without purpose and without hope. Thus Bodmer, another famous painter, wrote that when he came among the Plains tribes in the 1830's and 40's, he could leave his equipment for many days in any village or camp without fear of the least thing being touched, so honest were they. But when he came back in the 1880's much of this was changed. Drink and bad white men had corrupted the morals of these naive and innocent people so that nothing could be left unguarded anymore! How sad, how terribly sad. Out of this morass of despair, the modern Native Americans are only today beginning to pull themselves. Their chief help is a renewed belief in the value of much of what they have lost.

A similar and yet strikingly different story to that of the Winnebago Indian mentioned earlier in this chapter is found in a beautiful book called *When the Legends Die,* by Hal Borland (Bantam Books, 1965). Though fiction, it is much based on reality and has a tremendous punch.

In this story, George Black, a Ute of southern Colorado, kills or thinks he kills a man who robs him, but he is sure that the whites will hang him. So he secretly takes his wife and baby boy into the wilderness of the Rocky Mountains and tries to rebuild a home in the ancient way of his people. Both parents eventually die in the mountains, the man killed by an avalanche and the woman dying of tuberculosis, but they have taught the boy much of the old ways and the religion of his people. Knowing the ancient songs that were so important to the survival of the spirit, the boy gets along in the wilderness home comfortably with a grizzly cub for a pet.

The boy finally has to come down to civilization to get a new axe blade and other tools he needs, trading fine basketry he has made for the tools, but he is observed by Blue Elk, an old Ute who knows the boy will be worth money if he is brought back to the reservation. Blue Elk makes arrangements to be paid for getting the boy and goes after him, following his trail by clever tracking. When he finds the boy living in the old way and singing the beautiful old songs of the dawn, the sunset and others, he is temporarily overcome by nostalgia at the beauty of the old life way. He almost leaves the boy alone, but greed wins in the end, and he cleverly induces the boy to come out to civilization.

The boy innocently comes, thinking he is going to teach his people the old songs and the great things of their ancient culture, but he finds most of his people are following the white man's road and are uninterested in listening to him. He is hurt badly by this and other treatment they and the whites give him, but eventually is given a chance to ride horses and discovers that he is a natural at breaking wild horses. He is lured by a white man into being a paid bronc rider who rides in rodeos while his boss makes bets on him. The young man, Tom Black, pretends to ride poorly at first, fooling onlookers, but he then rides cleverly to win bets, all to his boss' profit.

This shoddy work is so degrading that the young Ute, not understanding the terrible loss he has suffered or why, turns in fury on the horses he rides and learns to ride some to their deaths until he becomes famous on the rodeo circuit as Killer Tom Black. At last, however, he is very nearly killed by a desperate horse that throws and tramples him. While in the hospital and recuperating, he begins to sort things out and finally realizes that he has to return to the wilderness to find what is missing in his life. So he goes back to the southern Colorado Rockies and takes a job as a lone sheepherder in the same area where he used to live in the mountains.

Gradually the beauty of the wild places, the high snow-covered peaks, the crystal-clear water tossing down the canyons, the meadows lovely with the pinks and golds, blues and scarlets of wildflowers, the dark coniferous forests mysteriously sighing in the wind, and the lovely white-barked quaking aspens, shimmering and flashing with light from their trembling leaves, begin to heal him. Once more he sings the old songs of the dawning, of the fire rising from the hearth of his crude shelter, of the sunset and evening, the stars and the moon, and the song of the hunt when he goes after a deer.

He meets again the great bear he once knew as a cub and a pet, but it has forgotten him and kills some of the sheep. Going after it with a gun deeper and deeper into the wilderness, he comes to a place he recognizes as ideal for a vision search and here, alone with Father Sky and Mother Earth and all the songs of nature, he finds the great cleansing he has so long sought.

It is a story of the broken pipe, symbolizing the broken life of a man, coming back to the Spirit again and fulfilling its meaning and its healing. It is sad, terribly sad that this book was made into a movie in which the significance of the whole story was lost despite some magnificent acting.

chapter FIFTEEN

Great Dreams Sent by the Above One

SONG TO THE PLEIADES

Look as they rise, rise,
Over the line where sky meets the earth;
Pleiades!
Lo! They ascending, come to guide us,
Pleiades,
Teach us to be, like you, united.

From *The Hako: A Pawnee Ceremony*. 22nd Annual Report, Bureau of American Ethnology, part 2, Washington, D.C., 1904, pages 13-372.

THE TRULY GREAT VISIONS OF the Native Americans are those in which they appear to rise above all local and narrow views of their own tribe or even of their own race and see the future of the world as a whole and all its peoples. It is wonderful that eventually they see all races, religions and nations coming into harmony and that there is no talk or dream of revenge against the whites for what they have done to the Indian people. In a way this bigness of vision means that they see that all of us on this earth are the children of the same Great Father Spirit and that, when our hearts are changed, when we become beautiful inside, then we will become true brothers and there will be justice for everybody regardless of race or background. In effect, the pride and vanity of each race will be destroyed and racial snobbery as a destructive thing will vanish to be replaced by love and understanding.

The vision of the old Makah

One of the most beautiful of these visions is that of the old Makah who in his ninety's told this remarkable story:

"When I was a little boy of five my father took me down to the edge of the sea at Neah Bay (the northwest tip Washington). He told me to put my hands down onto the sand and let the outermost waves coming in from the ocean lap over my hands. Then he told me: 'The spirit is going away from our people, from all the Indians, it is going up into the high mountains to hide for awhile. Our people are going to be split into little pieces by the white men, each part of us going different directions and acting lost for we will have no unity any more. This is a sad, sad thing for the Makah, we who have hunted the sea kings, the whales, since the beginnings. Our heroes of the past are weeping for us.

" 'So I want you to come down here to the edge of the sea every morning early as long as you live and I want you to pray for your people. Pray that the spirit will come back to them and you will recognize this spirit when it comes, for it will be big like this ocean that sends its waves in a great circle around the whole earth and sends its water in the form of rain into the hearts of all the lands. Remember now what I tell you and never forget and never neglect to come here and pray, for you will help that big thing come. When it comes, most people will not see it because they will be wrapped up in their own little troubles and likes and dislikes and beliefs; they will be too small at first to think big. But if you think big and listen big you will see this new thing and believe.

" 'After you have prayed, run up and down the beach as far as you can until you get too tired to run further, then wash yourself off and go home or to work. If you do this every day, you will become strong and healthy and you will live a long time until the big thing comes.' "

The vision of Black Elk

In the rolling grasslands of the Great Plains and under the sheltering wall of the Black Hills, the ancient Paha Sapa of the Sioux, the Cheyennes and other Plains tribes, there lived for many years a true holy man, Black Elk of the Oglala Sioux. This wonderful human being, pure of heart and a great teacher and healer somehow managed to keep alive in his heart and mind the beautiful essence of his people and their meaning in the Sacred Circle of earth and sky. He was born into the free life of the Plains peoples in 1863, but had his first great and extraordinary vision as a nine-year-old boy on the Great Plains near the Little Bighorn River in what is now Montana.

It is useless to give here details of this vision so finely described in the great book *Black Elk Speaks,* prepared by John Neihardt, but the outline given here may make you aware of the tremendous importance of learning about and understanding it.

High in the sky he was carried in his dream and up among the towering clouds to a beautiful tepee made of flaming rainbows where he met a council of six grandfathers who represented the Great Spirit. They told him he was being sent out across the sky to see the future of his people and the world. Riding a bay horse and followed by four troupes of horses, twelve in each troupe, one black, one white, one yellow and one red (whom I believe represented the four races of man), he started on his journey.

On this journey he saw repeatedly that though his people at the time of the dream were walking in the sacred way, under the flowering tree of their understanding and unity, they were soon to become sick in the spirit while great clouds and storms of darkness would surround and pummel them. Towards the end he saw them fleeing through a storm like frightened swallows, each voice crying alone and all unity lost. Later he was to understand that this great storm that broke and scattered his people was brought by the coming of the white people who conquered them, broke their spirit and filled their minds with so much conflict they indeed became lost.

Yet he was given the promise in his vision that something beautiful was coming and somehow the darkness would pass and a new day be born. He saw the Daybreak Star come from the east and with it a Sacred Being, all colored red, who turned into a bison, and he understood that though the buffalo would be lost to his people, something else equally good would take its place. He saw also that he would help bring back the spirit of his people and plant the Sacred Herb that grew up into a mighty Tree of Understanding, spreading its beautiful branches over the earth and filled with singing birds. Under this tree the Sacred Hoop of the Sioux, the symbol of their unity, but which had been broken, grew back together again. Then he saw many other hoops of other peoples and around them one great hoop that meant they had come into unity and understanding. Last he saw that the day was so beautiful that even the rocks and trees danced with joy in the glorious light, also the four-leggeds, the winged peoples and the two-leggeds.

The obvious meaning is that Black Elk saw in this vision the day when a glorious message of love and understanding and unity would bring the entire human race into the Sacred Circle of harmony with themselves and all living things. This can only be possible when something with tremendous spiritual power changes the hearts of mankind.

Black Elk also had a second great vision, which emphasized the meaning and power of the first. It happened when the Ghost Dance craze was shaking the Sioux nation and many other tribes in 1890. Many Plains Indians believed this dance, if properly done, would bring back the dead relatives to help them and would destroy the white people. The religion of the Ghost Dance had been started by a Paiute, called Wavoka, in Nevada, who actually taught a somewhat different message, which was that a new age would come only when all people came to love one another. He also taught harmony between the white race and the red, but the Indians of the Great Plains, hurt deeply by their conquest, had twisted this into hate. It was a time of much hunger and hardship for the Sioux in 1890, and Black Elk himself was seeking desperately for a way to bring back the spirit. Black Elk was uncertain about this dance, as he felt there was something not quite right about it, but he danced with the others, and in the midst of one dance at Wounded Knee Creek near Manderson, South Dakota fell into a faint, during which his vision came.

In his dream he was flying through the air following a spotted eagle which led him over a high dark ridge from which flames burst forth, but did not harm him. He soon came to a beautiful land of clear light, green grass and trees, singing birds, and many game animals. Below he saw six beautiful villages and to the sixth he came. Here he was met by twelve men who told him that a Sacred Being was there waiting for him. He was led into the village and, under the Sacred Tree which was blooming there with lovely flowers, he saw a man standing, wonderful in appearance, out of whose body rays of many colored light were pouring. This man had long black hair and looked like neither a white man nor an Indian, but he spoke to Black Elk, saying: "My life is such that all earthly beings and growing things belong to me. Your father, the Great Spirit, has said this. You too must say this." Then he disappeared like a puff of smoke. The twelve men then told Black Elk: "Behold them (meaning the people in the Sacred Land). Your nation's life shall be such!"

Soon Black Elk was carried back to the Ghost Dance where he reentered his sleeping body and came awake, finding his people around him, but the tree in the center of the circle was dead. He was dazed by this strange dream, and uncertain then and until the end of his life as to just what it meant. But he did believe that this Sacred Being he saw was the same One, painted red, he had seen in his first great vision, the one who brought the Sacred Herb back to the earth and caused it to grow into a great tree, the Tree of Understanding, under which all life came into harmony.

We can either think of this Sacred Being Black Elk speaks about as being on earth at the time he had the visions, or as yet to come. Either could be correct, as Jesus, for example, did not become widely known until at least two centuries after His passing and yet His Message shook the world.

The vision of the Wishram great great grandmother

The Wishram are a small tribe living in south central Washington mostly along the Columbia River. I have heard bits of this story from several Indians and am here trying to tie it together.

She who was very old and wrinkled, living in the last days of the winter of her life, opened her eyes like bright coals one day, like a last flash of the inner fire before the final sunset, and said to her great great grandchildren something like this:

"Many many winters have I seen since the days when I was a child and there was only the beautiful land and my own folk in it. I have seen the white people come like the locusts who cover the ground and destroy every blade of grass. I have seen my people forget the good things they once knew and become very foolish. I hear the young men now talking about hating the white people, but this is not the true spirit that is to come back. It is something much bigger!

"One day, I tell you with all my heart, one day the white people and the Indians will change, like the dead things of winter change into the beautiful green and the flowers of springtime. And in that day, when a new spirit power comes, they will become brothers and make the whole earth beautiful!"

A great vision of Crazy Horse, holy man and warrior of the Sioux

Crazy Horse was one of the main leaders of the Teton Sioux in their final battles against white encroachment on their lands in what are now the Dakotas, Montana, Wyoming and Nebraska. He was killed through treachery at Fort Robinson, Nebraska, in 1879 at the young age of about 36, but the last years of his life were spent in such dedicated service to his people that today a great monument in solid granite is being carved to his memory in the Black Hills of South Dakota. During those years he several times sought for visions to try to find the answer to why the white people were coming and destroying the old Indian culture and religion.

On Bear Butte in South Dakota, the Sacred Mountain of the Sioux and Cheyenne peoples, he had his great vision, about 1871. Details of the vision were given me by Frank Fools Crow, a medicine man of the Oglala Sioux. The full account of the vision is given in my book, *Great Upon the Mountain, Crazy Horse of America,* but here is a shortened version of it:

Crazy Horse went clear to the top of Bear Butte in the midst of summer to seek his vision, a brave thing to do in those days as the top was supposed to be highly dangerous with spirit power and the striking of lightning. At the top he laid down his buffalo robe over some sage-brush leaves and prepared for a long vigil.

On the evening of the third day a thunder storm came out of the west and lightning struck all around him, but did not kill him, and that night he had his vision.

In it he saw his people being driven into spiritual darkness and poverty while the white people prospered in a material way all around them, but even in the darkest times he saw that the eyes of a few of his people kept the light of the dawn and the wisdom of the earth, which they passed on to some of their grandchildren. He saw the coming of automobiles and airplanes, and twice he saw the great darkness and heard the screams and explosions when millions died in two great world wars.

But after the second great war passed, he saw a time come when his people began to awaken, not all at once, but a few here and there and then more and more, and he saw that they were dancing in the beautiful light of the Spirit World under the Sacred Tree even while still on earth. Then he was amazed to see that dancing under that tree were representatives of all races who had become brothers, and he realized that the world would be made new again and in peace and harmony not just by his people, but by members of all the races of mankind.

Chilam Balam, the Great Seer of the last days of the Maya, and his vision of the future of the world

The Mayan Indians probably produced the greatest civilization of America before the coming of the Europeans. Though still living in the Stone Age, because they had developed little use of metal, they yet produced a complex and beautiful culture. It was noted for its marvelous art and spectacular buildings and pyramids, and particularly for great advances in astronomy and mathematics, including probably the first invention of the zero, the most useful of all mathematical symbols. On top of this their culture developed during its early and great ages a harmony of peoples in which war was practically unknown and trade and other arts of peace and cooperation flourished over wide areas, a remarkable manifestation of a religion that obviously brought much unity and understanding.

In the dying days of the Maya culture at the close of the 15th century there appeared a famous seer and priest of the old religion of Quetzalcoatl, who wrote a great book of prophecy called *The Book of Chilam Balam*. Copies of this book in the Mayan language but in the Latin script were made by later Mayans who were educated by the Catholic priests, and then several translations of these were made into Spanish and then into English, of which the two most famous are *The Book of Chilam Balam of Tizimin,* and *The Book of Chilam Balam of Chumayel*. The second of these books shows a great deal of white-Christian influence and so I believe is not as authentic as the first named, in which Chilam Balam speaks as a true Mayan and criticizes the influence of the Christians as he sees it coming. Also in this book of Tizimin are found more of the prophecies.

His people speak of Chilam Balam with awe because of the marvelous exactness of his prophecies. He correctly warned them that after the coming of the white strangers, whom he foretold would land on the shores of Yucatan in 1517, they would have three great epidemics of sickness that would kill thousands. These were the smallpox epidemics, similar to those which hit the Native Americans everywhere and helped destroy their strength to resist the invaders. He also told of a great hurricane that would hit Yucatan in 1593 and destroy much life and property. These dates were given by aid of the famous Mayan calendar which is at least as accurate as our own Gregorian calendar.

He said that the great wheel of time, the Katun Wheel of 260 Mayan years, which makes one revolution in 256 of our years, would make a complete circle during which nothing but bad would come to the Indians. Toward the end he said would come the last Mayan revolt against their conquerors and this was one of the most amazing prophecies of all, for he said it would begin in 1847-48, which is when it did!

The three most mysterious prophecies come toward the end of the book but, since all the other prophecies came true, we should look at them with respect and investigate them carefully. These three prophecies not only promise the return of the ancient Mayan glory, but the coming of something bigger than this, a force, says Chilam Balam, destined to break down the walls of prejudice and misunderstanding between all peoples and bring them together in harmony and justice.

The first date he gives that is obviously the start of this coming unity, is 1862-63 because of the overlapping of the Mayan year with our own. Thus the Mayan year count of Katun 5 Ahau (a 20-year period), had a 12th tun (or Mayan year) that covered the last half of 1862 and the first half of 1863. At this time, prophesied Chilam Balam, one whom he called "the Lord" would arrive in "benign holiness." If true, a Great Being could have first proclaimed a message of unity to mankind in this year. If so, why did not this appear in our news media? The answer could be the same as in the time of Jesus. It took several centuries for His message to reach the outlying parts of Europe, and the people in power tried to ignore it or hide it for some time.

The second prophecy is just as strange as the first. It proclaims that in the 9th tun of Katun 5 Ahau, which would happen in the years 1868-69, that the "Lords" would be "imprisoned" and this would be a time of broken hearts (or broken pottery shards as the prophecy puts it in symbolic language). Again we can ask who was imprisoned and why? Perhaps the Holy Land would provide the answer as many prisoners of the Turkish Empire were imprisoned there at that time for religious and political reasons.

The third of these mysterious prophecies sets no date. But it is obviously based on the coming of the "Lord" or "Lords" already referred to when it says: "I say that the divisions of the earth shall all be one!'' In other words, a great Spiritual Force would come to the world which would eventually knock down all the walls between men and bring them together in unity. I believe we are already beginning to see the knocking down of the walls, even though there is much darkness yet, for world travel, world communication and good books that teach us to know and understand other peoples are increasingly bringing all the earth together in understanding, including more and more understanding of the need for world unity if we are to avert world destruction.

I think Chilam Balam echoes the promise in the Bible in *Isaiah* 60:1-3, where it says:

"Arise, shine, for your light has come, and the glory of the Lord has risen upon you. For behold, darkness shall cover the earth, and thick darkness the peoples, but the Lord will arise upon you, and His glory will be seen upon you, and nations shall come to your light, and kings to the brightness of your rising."

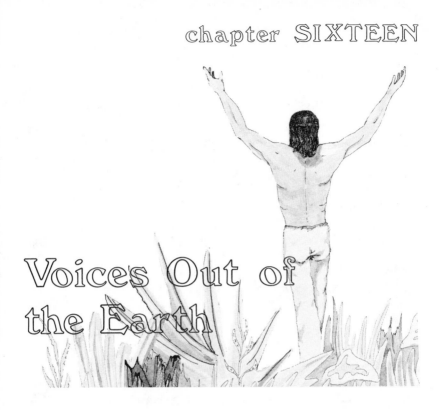

chapter SIXTEEN

Voices Out of the Earth

For even while I call myself poor,
Somewhere far off
Is one who is my Father,
Beseeching the breath of the divine one . . .
His life-giving breath,
His breath of old age,
His breath of waters,
His breath of seeds. . .
His breath of fecundity,
His breath of power,
His breath of strong spirit,
His breath of all good fortune whatsoever,
Asking for his breath,
And into my warm body drawing his breath,
I add to your breath,
That happily you may always live.
To this end, my fathers, my children,
May you be blessed with light.

From *Zuni Ritual Poetry*, by Ruth L. Bunzell. Bureau of American Ethnology, 47th Annual Report; 1932, page 701.

IN MY TRAVELS OVER AMERICA to visit Indian friends I have met many wonderful human beings who have expressed both in their words and in the quality of their lives a sense of wisdom and harmony with each other and with earth and sky. In telling some of their stories here, I do not wish to imply that these few are any better than many other fine people I have met, for I know many others equally filled with goodness. These are the accounts, however, that have particularly stayed with me and have special meaning and flavor. Of course all of these people have their faults, even as you and I, but here I am not speaking of these, but rather of those things that spur us on to better and wiser lives.

A Ute who taught humbleness

Eddie Box, Senior, Sun Dance Chief of the Southern Utes at Ignacio, Colorado, has always made me think of him as I would one of the great Indians of the old days. When I saw him dancing in the Sun Dance I felt his whole being partook of the nobleness and beauty of earth and sky. When I told him the story of my vision search on Bear Butte, he asked me quietly:.

"But did the door open when you climbed the mountain?"

"What do you mean about a door opening?" I asked.

"It is as if all of a sudden you seem to walk through a great door into a place of light!"

"No, this did not happen to me," I replied.

"It is supposed to happen to some who seek visions there," he replied. "That you have not seen the door may mean you still have a ways to go in your search."

He did not intend it, but I felt humbled that day, for I realized that I had acted proud of what I had seen on that mountain. It is good to be humble before both the Great Spirit and a Native American who has the wisdom of the old way.

Eddie invited me to take the sweat bath of purification with him and others of his friends. I helped him gather a lot of wood to build the big fire for heating the stones red hot. At the end of the sacred path that leads from the door of the sweat lodge towards the east he had placed an old buffalo skull, a sign he said of power of the Great Spirit. Unfortunately, when I came carrying wood for the fire, I walked between the sweat lodge and the buffalo skull.

"Come back around!" he commanded me quietly but firmly. "You must never cross in front of the sacred skull!" I did as he commanded, again humbled, for I should have known better. We must respect the sacred things of other people, regardless of whether we understand them or not, for these things have deep meaning to them.

In the sweat lodge, later, after prayers had been made to the spirit world, the water was thrown on the sacred hot rocks—sacred because they represent the power of Father Sun, and the steam that rises from them is the cleansing power of the spirit. As the steam got hotter and hotter until the temperature of the lodge rose to around 175 degrees F., I was forced to lower my head lower and lower until my nose was nearly touching the ground in efforts to find air to breathe. But even as we became hot and sweated, we chanted songs and prayers to the Great Spirit to cleanse not only our bodies, but also our minds of all harmful things. Four times the heat was raised up to a high degree and four times the door of the lodge was opened to let in light and air, symbolizing the four ages of the earth, and the four directions of harmony. After the sweat bath was over and we came out of the lodge I, the inexperienced one, was so weak and dizzy that I barely made it to the room where I was to recuperate. Where possible, after such ceremonies, you are supposed to throw yourself into cold water, but I had missed seeing the hose that was used for this purpose that dry hot evening.

The Cheyenne with the face that mirrored the wilderness

One time in 1965 John Stands-in-Timber, the well-known historian of the Cheyennes of Montana, who has already been spoken about in this book, took me and my wife and children to see Willis Medicine Bull, whom he described as a medicine man and a very wise man of his tribe. We found Medicine Bull living in a small but attractive house near Barney, Montana, not far from the banks of the Tongue River. I was instantly struck by his remarkably spiritual face. It was medium brown and wrinkled, framed by thick black hair that hung down his back in two long braids wrapped part way in sheaths of doeskin. But the singular ethereal wildness of that face made me want to look into it for hours, for it made me think of lost waterfalls singing in hidden canyons, and the way the White-throated Swifts waft like arrows of light across the blue sky, forever free and wild.

I felt as if I were living a hundred years or more ago on the Great Plains and was talking to an old medicine man of that time. This feeling was heightened by the fact that Medicine Bull could not speak English, and to hear the strange but enchanting sound of the old Cheyenne language coming from him was like being a part of the ancient days of the free plains, as if my naked body were wrapped in a buffalo hide with the hair against me. John Stands-in-Timber translated for me, and I remember asking Medicine Bull if he had ever heard of any prophecy of Sweet Medicine, the Cheyenne culture hero, which went beyond his prophecy of the coming of the white people and how they would destroy the Indian culture.

He was silent for a long time and I respected his silence. Finally he drew with a piece of stick on the floor and said, as translated:

"I have heard of no other prophecy of Sweet Medicine about this, but our brothers, the Suhtai, had a great hero, too, called Standing-on-the-Ground, he who brought the sacred buffalo hat, and he is said to have made a strange prophecy. He said that someday a Sacred Tree would come out of the east, and around this tree all peoples would come to dance, even the white people, and that would be a good time all over the world."

For a long time I gazed at that mysterious and beautiful face, while John Stands-in-Timber talked to him and questioned him, sometimes translating bits of conversation into English, but at last Medicine Bull raised his hand to indicate that he was tired, and I left the old man with great regret.

A wise and humble Hopi chief

There is something about the Hopi people that is very hard to explain. Perhaps it is part of the secretiveness thrust upon them by the white people's attempts to change them to fit the standards of western culture. Of course there are some Hopis who have followed the white man's way, though I suspect that even they continued to carry within themselves much of the Hopi road. But I feel it is fortunate that many Hopi still refuse to worship a mechanistic civilization or to recognize the value of a culture which justifies the ruthless exploitation of nature by man. Instead, they continue to point out that by exploiting nature without understanding it, man has indeed cut himself off from the Great Mystery that he calls God, and is in danger of destroying the very earth whose resources he once thought inexhaustible.

David Monongye, a chief of the newest Hopi village, Hotevilla, has visited us at our home and we have visited him at his. His home, a simple adobe dwelling, like those of the ancient ones of his people, had neither electricity nor running water at the times of our visits, but expressed in its rich brown color, and the hand-made artifacts together with the drying corn of its interior, the love of Mother Earth and her fruits that is so characteristic of the Hopi. But this "in-tuneness" with Mother Earth has not been sufficient in modern times to make the Hopi in tune with each other. Their spirit is broken, as is ours, into several mutually exclusive divisions, sometimes antagonistic. And this was the one thing that most bothered my old and wise friend David Mononogye, when I talked to him.

"We have picked up too many of the feelings of the white people," he said. "Even as they are divided by walls, so are we, and we do not know yet how to get rid of this burden. Hopi have withstood torture and imprisonment in protest against the white man trying to force us into his way, but other Hopi laughed at us for our efforts. Our ancestors told us that a very bad time would come when we saw white streaks across the sky (the streaks of jet planes), and when a black ribbon (the modern highway) would cross our land from end to end. Both of these things have happened and now indeed we are having trouble. The worst bad thing is the destruction of our land by the big shovels (speaking here of the strip-mining in the Southwest to get coal for electric generators), and the coming of the dark cloud (smog) over our beautiful mesas."

"But what," I asked him, "of the Hopi prophecy that one day we will have a beautiful new world?"

"Yes, that will come when the True Brother comes out of the east, and when the Blue Star Kachina dances in the *kisonvi* (central square of the village) for the first time. Then will a new and powerful spirit spread over the land."

I knew that the Blue Star Kachina, like others called by this name, was an earth spirit who acted as a messenger, taking the prayers of the people to the Great Spirit. Symbolically he appears to the people in the form of a Kachina doll or as a Kachina dancer in one of the ceremonies.

After we sat for a while in silence, I said:

"We will pray that this time comes soon before our present civilization destroys the earth, but let us watch carefully, for this new thing may come differently than you or I or anyone expects."

He nodded his head slowly in agreement.

Two wise and kind ladies

There are many wonderful and wise Indian women I have met, though sometimes I see in their faces the imprint of years of suffering and privation. I have also seen some extremely fine dancers, and the stately, noble way they dance expressed to me deep character and a beautiful spirit. So I wish I had room to tell about all these very fine ladies and express my appreciation for their many acts of kindness, for the good warmth of their presence and the wisdom I have learned from them. I hope all will understand how my heart feels, and forgive me that I mention only two on these pages.

Up near the mouth of the Klamath River, that wild and mighty river that pours out of the high mountains of northwestern California, I long ago met Florence Shaugnessy of the Yurok people. Like many of this people in modern times, she has some Irish background, as a number of Irish settled here in pioneer times and married into the Yurok tribe.

"Really," I told her, "this is a good combination, as among the peoples of Europe, I believe the Kelts, and particularly the Irish Kelts, were closest of all in spirit to the Native Americans. They were an earth and sky people in the old days, and often they sang of the spirits of the earth, the little people, or elves and fairies."

"We also believe in the little people," she laughed, "and many other things most modern people laugh at."

Then, while seated in that warmly peaceful room beautifully decorated with ancient Indian crafts, I told her of some of the strange experiences I had had with the Indian peoples and the remarkable things I had seen. And I asked her, "Tell me of what you saw in the old days."

"When I was a girl," she replied, "we used to have the New Salmon ceremony at the mouth of the Klamath River near here, and we felt that this ceremony, when well done, brought in large numbers of salmon to be dried and smoked to keep us alive through the dark cold winters. In those times the old medicine man would call all the young strong men to move a particularly large rock that stood on the beach. They would push and struggle and puff and strain, but even several of them working together could not move it. Then the old man would say a prayer, step up to the rock, put his hand on it and move his whole body in a peculiar way, as if somehow he was part of the universe, and the rock would move over where he wanted it! Then and only then could the New Salmon ceremony begin."

"That is beautiful," I said, "and I, too, believe in that power. Now please tell me more of the old days."

"My mother," she said, "was a wonderful woman with much knowledge of the earth and its life, how to heal, and many other things. I am so sorry I did not learn all I could from her, but now she is gone! One time when I was about eleven she was boiling some seafood in a large cauldron, and somehow I came in in a hurry, bumped the cauldron and spilled boiling water all down my front! I started screaming, but my mother just calmly poured some cold water into a bowl, said a prayer over it for an instant, sucked as much of the water as she could up into her mouth, and sprayed me all over where I had been badly scalded. A most wonderful thing happened then. The pain instantly disappeared, and I was completely well within a few hours. How much I wished I had learned from her this secret, for many years later, after she was dead, I was scalded again in a similar way, and all the salves I put on those burns could help me only partly. I was many days getting well. So did the old people know many secrets we have lost!"

The other lady I would like to speak about is Mrs. Elsie Allen, a Pomo of Ukiah. She has almost seemed like a mother to me because she is so kind and good. She was also very patient when I came to take close-up photographs of her beautiful basket work, including the famous Pomo feather baskets, with the brilliantly colored feathers of the orioles, meadowlarks, woodpeckers, flickers and mallard ducks. Twice I have taken her and her friends on trips to gather willows and sedge roots to make these baskets, and learned at first hand of the infinitely patient and careful work needed to first collect these raw materials, then split, dry and shave them into the proper shape for baskets. It is amazing to see this spry old lady down on her hands and knees or seated on the ground, prying and digging away to get the long dark roots of the sedge plant, found usually near creek banks. But it is a merry, happy time, as I am sure it must have been in the old days too, taking part in this fine outdoor constructive work to help make creations of beauty and usefulness. All laugh, particularly when one is pulling hard at a root and it comes out too suddenly, and all exclaim with joy when any one of the diggers finds a particularly good root for a basket.

But Elsie has told me much about her young days when life was often very difficult for an Indian girl, yet she speaks calmly about it, and without hard feelings.

"I was taken," she told me, "when I was about eleven to a government school at Covelo on the Round Valley Indian Reservation. At the time I could hardly speak any English, but they would not let me speak in my own language or anybody else talk to me in that language. They seemed to expect me to learn, whether I knew English or not! Almost the entire time at this school was lost because nobody took time to really teach me anything. When I think of all the other Indian boys and girls that were treated this way in those days, coming to strange schools and being treated like little animals, it makes me weep!"

Truly, love and understanding was needed then and is needed now between all peoples.

Mad Bear on Indian youth

Recently Mad Bear Anderson, well-known Tuscarora medicine man and Iroquois leader from the State of New York, came to visit us at our home. I have known Mad Bear for some years and always greatly enjoyed seeing him, as he has a great deal of wisdom, a fine sense of humor, and is just plain delightful to be around. One time Mad Bear went swimming with me and the other friends in the Gualala River. But, when he dived in, much of the pool was thrown out on the banks! So you can understand he is a big man! He is a big man in the spirit also, and this is what he said when I asked him what he thought was happening to Indian youth today:

"The year 1967 seems to me to be the turning point for Indian youth, for that year they began more than ever before to return to traditional Indian values. Previous to that our young people, for the most part, had no desire for such things, having brush cuts to their hair and being disdainful of the old culture, for they were following all the fads of the white young people. But we have long had a legend that one day the Indian would begin to come back to his own, and it was told that for a long time before this happened the Indian grandfathers and grandmothers would symbolically be like part skeletons, lying half-buried in the earth, mostly just bones with only part of the flesh left, although there seemed to be a throb still as their hearts barely beat to keep them still alive. However, the legend told us how in time our young people would begin to search for the old spirit and the old ways and become proud of them again. As they began this search, they would try to get wisdom from their grandfathers and grandmothers. So they would begin to work very hard, talking to everybody they could, including the few medicine men that still were active, and any of the old ones still able to remember the past. This then began to put flesh back onto the old bones, and, in doing this, the youth neglected to cut their hair so it began to grow long again, as it was in the old times.

"During the six years since 1967 the Unity Caravan has also been started by the Indians in New York to travel all around and help revive the spirit. Many young Indians who had laughed at such things before, began to travel with this caravan, which carried dances, songs and beautiful ceremonies to all parts of the country.

"We were told in the legend that one day a Choice Seer, a young Indian from among us, would stand up before us and unite our people, and that he would speak to many other people also about unity and understanding. So now it is true that the young people are pushing the old people out of their graves of the spirit and helping bring them back to the great things of the past, both old and young helping each other. We are also learning where the safe places are to be when the forces of nature begin to cleanse the earth of all the destruction, pollution, greed and selfishness of our present civilization. It will be a terrible cleansing, but necessary, and then the New Age of Man shall come."

Photo of Bear Butte, South Dakota. *Courtesy of Bear Butte State Park.*

chapter SEVENTEEN

Preparing for a Vision Search on Bear Butte

"Hear me, four quarters of the world—
A relative I am!
Give me the strength to walk the soft earth,
A relative to all that is!
Give me the eyes to see and the strength to understand,
That I may be like you.
With your power only can I face the winds."

From *Black Elk Speaks,* arranged by John Neihardt. Univ. of Nebraska Press, 1961.

OH BEAR BUTTE, OH BEAR BUTTE—I hear you calling in my dreams. From the swelling green waves of grass of the Great Plains in summer I see you lifting towards the sky, like the great hump of the Grizzly Bear. Alone and solitary are you, a separate relative to your cousins that are the Paha Wapa, the Black Hills. Though you are not too high, there is something about you different from all other mountains, for you cast the spell of a strange and brooding spirit, a power out of the earth, a head reached to Father Sky, and a challenge to all that is false and harmful to the living world. From you I pray shall continue to come visions to shake mankind.

It is hard to explain the thrill this mountain has on men and women who sense its spirit. The first I heard about Bear Butte was from the Cheyennes at Lame Deer, Montana, but it seemed even that day as if the mountain had been merely sleeping in my heart. From the Indians you could hear the reverence for it ringing in their words.

East from the Pacific Ocean I came in the summer of 1966, seeking for Bear Butte, but seeking also for Frank Fools Crow, holy man of the Oglala Sioux, the man, who for me I knew, had the key of the Sacred Mountain. With me came my son, Keven, age 8, my daughters, Roxana, 12, Tamara 14 and four teen-age boys of high quality.

There is something that expresses the essense of the Sioux as they used to be and as some still are in the high plains of western South Dakota. A land of rolling hills and small river valleys, sprinkled with a few buttes and with the great wild jagged stretch of the Badlands to the north, beaten by the hot sun of summer and the rains from the thunderheads that roam in out of the west, and torn and smothered by the cold snowy blizzards of winter, this is a land of extremes. So were the Sioux once ferocious warriors, fighting for their beloved earth, and yet, when you got to know them, beautiful with human warmth and appreciative of every living thing. So have I found some of them in this time, those craggy faces that bespeak a warrior past and yet also that steadfast look that tells of honor and purity. So did the old Sioux lady tell me once: "There are a few yet whose hearts touch the clouds and whose feet feel the meaning of the earth!" And most of them will come back to this, I feel sure!

I was glad to see Fools Crow again, and also his son-in-law, Enos Lone Hill, who translated for him. At first it was a time for long silences and short talks, but Frank was all smiles and greeted us with pleasure. I brought with me a pipe bag of the Oglala Sioux (see illustration), which had been given my father, Dr. Henry Alexander Brown, when he was a young country doctor treating sick Sioux people at the Pine Ridge Reservation in 1895. I told Fools Crow how my father had healed a young boy, a son of an Oglala Sioux chief, of pneumonia, and had refused payment because he saw how badly the Sioux were being treated at that time. But the father of the boy had insisted on giving my father this bag. I explained how after my father had told me the story of this bag when I was five years old, I had repeatedly had a strange and wonderful dream (see *Warriors of the Rainbow,* by William Willoya and Vinson Brown, Naturegraph Publishers), in which I saw the Indian people rise from their misery on a dark earth into a glorious sky of light where they were dressed in the beautiful way and were singing the old songs.

The old man held, touched and looked at the bag with great reverence, pointing out that the two red crosses on its beaded surface represented the good red road of the four directions that lead to purity and glory if one follows the right path in life. He then asked me: "This is a Sacred Bag of our people and very old. Will you return it to us?"

"This bag was given to my father," I replied "because the chief who gave it to him said he had had a dream in which he was told to give it to the first white man who helped his family without asking a return, and that someday this would bring good to the Indian peoples. Therefore, this bag was given to my family for a purpose. If I am told by the Great Spirit to return it now or any other time to your people, then I shall be glad to do so. But meanwhile I will be glad to loan you the bag for a year and let you examine it and use it in ceremonies. I would like to know where it originally came from and who owned it."

Taking the bag very carefully, he laid it back in its wooden case, one that had been made for me by a father of one of the boys who was along on this trip, Mr. James Grant, of Healdsburg, California.

"Thank you," he said, "I will be very careful of this. When not being used, we will keep it in the safe at the Pine Ridge Reservation Headquarters."

We sat for a while in silence feeling the warmth of the summer sun and watching some swallows darting and dashing after insects above his home. At last I spoke again.

"I have come this summer to ask you to help me go on a vision search, a Hanblecheyapi, on Bear Butte."

"This is a very serious thing," he replied. "Bear Butte is sacred to us and has great power. To seek a vision there without proper preparation and without purity of heart could lead to something very bad, even early death. We are having an Inipi ceremony, a healing ceremony here, in a few days. We can also use this as a purifying ceremony. If you will come to my house that evening, we can determine whether you will be ready this year for the Hanblecheyapi, the vision search."

At the time promised, we were staying with some friends at Interior, South Dakota, near Park Headquarters for Badlands National Monument. I left my daughters and two of the youth who were with me with these friends for the afternoon and evening, and learned later that Roxana entertained them all royally at the piano while we were gone. The other two youths, Tom Grant and Randy Ristau, along with Keven, my son, accompanied me to the Inipi Ceremony.

Arriving at Frank Fools Crow's home we found a group of Indians already gathered and introduced ourselves. Enos Lone Hill, Frank's son-in-law, was there, and invited us to have a stewmeat dinner before the Inipi began. When it was time for the Inipi to begin about eight o'clock that evening, he explained what was to be done. He said we would all form a big circle in the main room of the house, holding hands, except for Frank and Enos, who would be beating the drum. If everybody present had full faith in the healing and the purifying, he said, this would help greatly in making the whole ceremony a success. But he said if there was somebody present who had doubts or who had bad thoughts this could cause the little lights to turn orange, instead of their usual blue color, and then that person might suffer great harm. A young white man who had come to a similar ceremony some months before, he said, had committed suicide within a week after his visit, and that evening the lights had been orange, so evidently his thoughts had been wrong.

When we formed the circle, Enos pointed out to me about three people present who were suffering from some ailments and so had come to be healed, but he said there might be more. As we all held hands, Enos began to beat the drum softly, while Fools Crow, with braided hair topped by an eagle's feather, laid out on the central floor of the room his paraphernalia. This included an old buffalo robe on which he placed two rattles, some more eagle feathers, and a buckskin bag that contained his medicine. Some of the things from this bag he also laid out on the robe, but unfortunately I have forgotten what they were, though I seem to remember a number of small colored stones. This medicine bag and its contents are usually determined by the medicine man from a vision he has had about them, and only then do they take on sacred and healing meaning. Actually there is a great deal of psychotherapy about such a ceremony as I was about to experience, in which the sick person, if he truly believes, is healed by the power of the mind and the spirit.

Fools Crow then spoke to us in Sioux and Enos Lone Hill translated, saying that we were to observe absolute silence, to purify our minds of all thoughts save those of spiritual things, to hold hands and, especially during the time of darkness, to never let go. If anybody let go, the person whose hand felt the other let go was to shout out. Since there was no electricity in the house, the lights would all go out when the kerosene lanterns were snuffed out.

Then Fools Crow said a long prayer in Sioux, while the drum beat very softly, next he began to sing while the drum began to beat harder. Gradually the lights were snuffed out until we were all in complete darkness. Now the rattles seemed to float up off the floor and moved up near the ceiling, the latter about ten feet high. As they moved about rattling, a beautiful song was sung that went on and on.

Finally the rattles sank down to the floor again but continued rattling softly, and suddenly I was conscious of a light in the room. It was a very tiny blue light, like that made by a firefly, and I remember having a feeling of great exhileration because it was blue. It danced about and soon there was another one and another one also dancing, until the room seemed full of these little lights moving about. One came within six inches of my face and seemed to hover briefly, while I breathed deeply and kept my mind concentrated on the spirit. Then I noticed that these lights would dash from the floor of the room clear to the ceiling, and around to every corner. When one of them came close to the face of someone in the room, I would see that face outlined for a second in a pale ghostly glow, and especially a dark Indian face would take on a look of brooding mystery. By this time I was very happy indeed, for all lights were blue, not a single one orange, and there seemed to be great joy in the lights dancing to the beat of the drum. I cannot explain how this phenomena was done other than by a spiritual way, though I am sure my mechanistically minded friends may try to explain it to be some kind of rigging of wires and battery-run lights, but if so it would have been quite an expensive thing to contrive, as those little lights moved about everywhere with the utmost ease and there was never the slightest sign of anything attached to them. In fact, the dancing lights kept moving about right up to the time the signal was given to light the kerosene lanterns again, and when the big lights came on, I could see no sign anywhere of any wires.

The ceremony ended with a formal prayer by Fools Crow, and afterwards the room broke up into talking groups. I managed to get over to Fools Crow and ask him if any orange lights might have come, but he smiled and said "none!" Then I asked him if I could do the vision search on Bear Butte that summer, but he answered that he felt I needed a year of prayerful preparation and purifying and that the best time to go was next June 17-20, the height of the sun's journey to the north, when the good power of the Spirit on the mountain would be greatest and nature also would be at its strongest following the spring rains. So I agreed to come see him at that time.

Enos Lone Hill told me just before I left that Frank wanted me to pray for him too, during the year, so that both of us would have the best possible spirit power for the vision search. He also told me that Frank had been very pleased with me and the three white boys, as all had kept their spirits in harmony with the ceremony. He said much good would come from this for all of us.

After this ceremony, we travelled elsewhere in the Dakotas, but came back to the Pine Ridge Reservation at the town of Pine Ridge to watch the Sun Dance of the Oglala Sioux. Hundreds of Sioux and also whites interested in the ceremony came to camp by the Sun Dance grounds and attended. The Sun Dance in ancient days was usually put on by one of the leading men of the tribe to fulfill a promise he had made to the Great Spirit that he would dance in the sun dance and be pierced if a relative was saved from sickness or other trouble. Also those who danced in the Sun Dance did so to be a sacrifice to the tribe and through their ordeal to win help from the Lord of Being for their people.

In the old days the dancers were pierced with a sharp knife through the muscles of the back or the chest. In both cases thongs were put through the wound, but in the first case were tied to a buffalo skull that the dancer dragged around until the cord broke through his flesh or he fainted, while in the second case the long thongs were tied to the Sun Dance pole, which represented the Sacred Tree of Life. In this case, too, the thongs had to break loose from the flesh. Frequently the dancers would stare directly into the sun so that through this suffering too, they might receive visions while dancing. In the modern Sun Dance the dancers at Pine Ridge were pierced through the skin instead of the muscle, which is far less painful.

At this particular Sun Dance I was most startled to hear it announced over the loud speaker that the Sioux had discovered that the pipe bag that had been given to my father had actually once been the pipe bag of Crazy Horse and therefore was a very Sacred Bag! It was hung on the central Sun Dance pole and employed also in the ceremonies to touch the dancers and give them power.

I was even more surprised to have Fools Crow tell me after the Sun Dance was over that Crazy Horse's pipe bag had been given to my family for a great purpose, and that we were to keep it and guard and use it only in sacred ways. This we intend to do.

When I got home from our trip I began a series of special prayers every day to help my mind and heart be ready for the ordeal to come the following summer. Then, in the spring of 1967, about two months before I planned to leave for South Dakota, I had a most extraordinary vision that came completely unannounced one night in my sleep. As to the difference between an ordinary dream and a vision, the latter, in my experience, is usually almost startlingly clear and has about it a kind of magic aura of both suspense and excitation, so that what follows clearly takes on the feeling of a most meaningful message.

In this vision I was standing on what looked like the Great Plains with their waving green and yellow grasses, looking up at the sky. About two hundred yards above me appeared what looked like a small floating island with a flat top. On this surface Indians were dancing. They were most beautifully dressed in feathers, beads and skins in the ancient way and there was something about the way they danced that made me sure it was a sacred dance, for it had about it a feeling of great power and solemnity.

Seeing them, I was suddenly overcome by a strong fear. The fear stemmed from the fact that I realized these were holy men and women, and I felt myself stained by my weaknesses, knowing that if they wished, they had the power to look into my heart and mind and see all that was there. I wanted to crawl underground and hide!

Then I sensed that it was a dance of great spiritual joy, so strong that a new sensation came over me, that of intense longing to be up there dancing with them, attended by equally poignant sorrow as I realized that there was no way for me to pass up through that space to reach them. I stood there, tears running down my face, as I realized my helplessness.

Then, incredibly, I felt as if a great wind rushed upon me and carried me right up into the sky. I was put down on the edge of the island and a man stopped dancing and came to greet me, his face smiling, a most kind and friendly look in his eyes. Waving his arm he urged me to join in the dance and I did, watching carefully the steps of the others and copying them. But almost at once I was again overcome by a dark feeling of shame, so that once more I wished I were hidden under the earth. For I saw that, though the dancers were dressed in the beautiful way of old, both men and women, I was trying to dance among them completely naked! I was so ashamed!

The man who had greeted me earlier stopped dancing and came over to me, smiling as before, but this time with laughter in his eyes. From under his arm he unfolded a buckskin wrapping, taking out of it a costume as beautiful as any of the others. He invited with a wave of his hand that I dress myself in it and continue the dance. This I quickly did and felt overcome almost instantly with joy. Now my dance was like that of the antelope in the springtime and I felt completely accepted by these wonderful people and part of the sacred circle. With this most glorious feeling still lingering, I shortly thereafter awoke.

This was, it seems to me, a vision of my whole life with its ups and downs of spiritual progress, losses or retreats. My trail of life has not yet reached the last part of that vision, for I still feel inadequate and incomplete, but I pray that this vision will be fulfilled!

chapter EIGHTEEN

When Fire
Rimmed the Sky

For ages and ages the plans have been made.
For ages and ages the plans of the Sacred Mountains have been made.

—Origin Legend of the Navajo

From page 50 of *Navajo Wildlands*, Sierra Club, Ballantine Books, 1969.

THIS EVENING I HIKED UP into the hills behind our small ranch and looked across the valleys to distant peaks. They were only small mountains compared to the Rockies or the Sierras, and very tiny compared to the Himalayas, but still they had the magic of all mountains about them, the magic of wildness, of being somehow separated from man's civilization, at least until he builds roads up them. But even some of these mountains I can see from our hills have no roads up them and so they are sanctuaries, sanctuaries from the noise and the clamor, the rush, rush of many bodies, and the walls of steel and concrete. The time we shall need these sanctuaries desperately is coming soon, the time when mankind—exhausted and terrified by the death of the spirit his reckless search for progress, power, wealth, and pleasure has brought—will seek once more the wilderness and its Creator, from whence alone comes the strength to rebuild the world in beauty.

It is a beauty not only of outer things we need—the mountains, the waterfalls—but a beauty of inner things as well, the inner spirit—calm, collected, controlled—thinking thoughts like the rainbow, drinking at the clear spring of love and spreading it to the world. And both kinds of beauty need each other to exist, for they are really one.

So in the summer of 1967 I drove east again from California to the high plains of South Dakota, through the sacred hills, the Black Hills, the Paha Sapa, and on to the northeast of them, to Paha Tonka Wah-on-ksee-cha, the most sacred mountain of all, Bear Butte. But on the way I stopped to see Fools Crow and make my last preparations before I climbed to the top of that peak where I would both seek a vision and expect an ordeal.

I had brought with me my son, Keven, again, now nine, my oldest daughter, Tamara, fifteen, and a young man named David Moore, who also longed to seek a vision, but did not know whether Fools Crow would accept him. He would not come with me to see Fools Crow, saying: "If it is meant to be that I make a search for a vision, let it come in a way I do not know." So I left him, Keven and Tamara with the friends at Interior, South Dakota, while I went south and west alone to find Fools Crow.

When I came to his home I took out my Sacred Pipe and carried it to his door. His wife let me in, and I came into the living room where Fools Crow was seated on a chair, smiling and nodding in welcome. I handed him my pipe, bowl forward, and said: "I have come to cry for a vision, the Hanblecheyapi, and here is my pipe. Please make it sacred so that I can take it to the top of the sacred mountain and seek a vision."

He took the pipe carefully in his hands, looked it over, and asked me if I had had a dream about it. I explained that I had and that the dream told me how to carve and paint it. He then took three large eagle feathers and tied them to it in place of the smaller eagle feathers I had used first, and tied also to it a tiny wrapped ball of the skin of a buffalo calf that he said made it one with the earth, while the feathers made it one with the sky. Then he took some sweet grass, sacred to the Sioux, and burnt the grass with a match, making a fragrant odor and passing the smoke back and forth over the pipe, while he said a little prayer in Sioux. Then he filled the pipe bowl with tobacco, lit it and smoked to the seven directions, west, north, east and south, up to Father Sky, down to Mother Earth, and then from the Great Spirit to his inner being. Now he handed the pipe to me and I also smoked it to the seven directions.

"Washtai! (that is good!)" he said.

I then presented him with the gifts I had brought—twenty-five sacks of Bull Durham tobacco—and showed him that I had with me strips of cloth of the four colors, black, red, yellow and white.

"Now," he told me, "you must find four sticks about four feet long, and as straight as you can, of the wild cherry. These you will use for the four directions when you go to the top of the mountain."

I decided that somehow this was a very unusual test. I went out to gather the cherry wood sticks, including four extra ones, for suddenly I had an idea.

After the sticks were gathered and trimmed, we started on our way. The trip, fortunately, went by Interior, but when I reached the place where Keven, David and Tamara were staying, the friends said they had gone on a hike into the Badlands, and my heart fell. You see I was counting on getting David to come too, as I felt he was a very pure soul and needed the search too.

As we drove north on the crooked road out of the Badlands on the way to Bear Butte, I suddenly saw a tiny figure detach itself from the mouth of a narrow canyon to our right. I slowed to a stop and turned to Fools Crow while pointing at the figure.

"I think that is one of my party, David Moore. He is a very fine young man, but too shy to ask you if he also could go on the vision search. Could you wait and see him and let me know if he can go?"

Fools Crow nodded his head.

Soon David came close and behind him trailed my daughter Tamara, and son, Keven. When they arrived and I introduced them, I saw Fools Crow give David Moore a long careful piercing look. David has a very frank and open face, a very kind face and often a merry one. He laughed as he told about their adventures exploring the canyon, and climbing through caves in the rocks. Suddenly Fools Crow nodded his head at me. So I spoke to David:

"Fools Crow says you can go on the vision search with us, if you would like!"

So it was that we took the two children back to our friends at Interior, where David got himself quickly ready to go on the quest, and I laughingly told him that I had already picked out his sacred prayer sticks for him in hopes he could go.

We were soon on our way again, driving by way of Rapid City and Sturgis to Bear Butte State Park. It was June 17, 1967, and a stunningly beautiful summer day, with the Great Plains that surrounded the Butte like a green emerald carpet, and the mountain itself glowing in the sunlight, the green of its slopes marked by dark clumps of yellow pine and wild mountain mahogany. I noted it had two peaks, the one to the east somewhat lower than the one to the west. Fools Crow told us we would climb the highest peak for our vigils, each selecting separate places on the top so we would not disturb each other.

On the way to the Butte we had stopped at a large store in Rapid City where each of us purchased a new blanket, a new wooden bowl and some fruit to put in the bowls as an offering to the Spirit. It was important, Fools Crow stated, to be able to wrap ourselves with blankets unused by any other person when we were on top of the Butte. He also told us some stories about the Butte, emphasizing that most Indians in the past had sought visions on the lower part of the Butte because of the danger from lightning when summer storms struck the mountain. But Crazy Horse, he said, was probably the first man to seek a vision on the highest top of the mountain. He explained that he himself, when much younger, had gone to the top alone seeking a vision, but these were the only persons who had done this so far as he knew.

It was about five o'clock in the afternoon when we reached a picnic place about a third of the way up the side of the Butte, and were happy to find there a small stream tossing down over the rocks and singing its gurgling song. So far as we could see there was no one else on the mountain that lovely day, and the sound of the water, the whispering of the wind in the pines and the liquid songs of the meadowlarks lower down on the grassy slopes were the only sounds we heard. All about us was a feeling of warm peace under a brilliantly clear blue sky.

It was here that Fools Crow made the final pipe ceremony, using his own pipe, and blowing smoke to the seven directions, then passing it so we each could take a puff. He then passed his pipe to David to use on the mountain top, as I had my pipe. He now directed us to walk up the mountain in a prayerful manner, adding ruefully that it was too steep for him to go this time, as he was too old and had arthritis. We must keep the pipestems always pointing to the front of us, he said and keep our minds and hearts wholly on the Spirit while going up, while at the top and while coming down. We were to stay at least twenty-four hours—longer if necessary, up to four days and nights—until we had visions. While up there we would have neither water nor food. At the top we could make widely separate beds out of the backpack full of sagebrush that I would carry, place in the ground our sacred sticks to the four directions and tie to the top of each stick a small flag of colored cloth, white for the north, yellow for the east, black for the south, and red for the west. Then each of us would take some of the sacred tobacco and sprinkle it in a sacred circle around our place of vigil, and place outside this circle the bowl containing the offering of fruit. Last we would each take off our clothes, each wrap himself in a blanket, placing the clothes outside the circle, for nothing of metal must be inside the circle. After doing this, we would each hold the sacred pipe with the stem pointing toward the west, say a prayer or sing a song to the Spirit, asking for help for our people and that we might better serve them, each time pointing the pipe to the seven directions and asking for a vision, then move back to the center again, before going out next to the north, then to the east and finally to the south before starting all over. The whole circle was to be done quite slowly.

On the way up the mountain beautiful butterflies danced around us, dragonflies came flitting over to look at us curiously from their haunts along the brook, and ground squirrels popped into their holes when we got close to them. Up through the pines we went, the trail winding steeply with a series of natural rocky stairs, like climbing a sacred stairway into the sky. At last we reached the saddle between the two peaks and paused here to rest but a moment before the last ascent.

At the top I spread out two beds of sagebrush at widely separated points so we would not interfere with each other's lonely vigil, but I found that no matter where I put the sagebrush there were plenty of sharp rocks sticking up underneath and that I really did not have enough sagebrush. There were a few yellow pine trees on the top, but the view was like that from an airplane looking down on the whole earth below. Bear Butte was a truly lonely peak in the midst of the Great Plains, but with the vast masses of the Black Hills looming off to the southwest like myriad dark bear backs. In all other directions the Plains extended in emerald green waves, lovely as the first morning of the world.

We were out of sight of each other, alone on the mountain top, and each proceeded with the last preparations for the vigil. I sprinkled a circle of tobacco around my chosen spot, symbolizing the Sacred Circle of Earth and Sky, of All Life, and of Mankind, put the plain wooden bowl and its fruit offering outside, and then stripped off my clothes and placed them outside the circle too. Wrapping the new blanket about me, I took my Sacred Pipe in one hand with the stem pointing outward and began my prayer and song circle, first to the west, then to the north, east and south, in a slow procession, like that of the equinoxes. As I walked out to each point of the compass, I sang an ancient Sioux song I had memorized, "Wakan-Tanka—Onshimala ye oyate wani wachin cha!": (meaning "Oh Great Spirit, be merciful to me that my people may live!"). Then I would point the stem of the pipe to each of the four main directions, saying at each direction a new prayer, then up to Father Sky, down to Mother Earth (two symbols, male and female, of the same Supreme Being), and then from the sky into the seventh direction, my own center, drawing the Spirit to me.

In the prayers I emphasized my own insignificance, no more important than the smallest ant, helped only if my heart became purified and the Spirit entered. I determined that my crying for a vision would not be for myself, but for all the peoples of the world, so I would be one of many instruments working to bring all races, religions and nations together in harmony. Knowing how easy it was to let the mind wander, but how absolutely vital it was to keep it directed to the Spirit, I decided I would keep up a rhythm that would keep it always occupied in a spiritual way. I had heard too often of those who failed because for a moment they lost sight of their goal, so I determined strongly never to falter even for a second. I felt I had too much at stake; as all the spiritual failures and foolish deeds of my life had somehow to be made up for by this vigil on the mountain top, crying not only for a vision to help the world but also for forgiveness and cleansing.

I knew that while up there I had to watch carefully the life about me, the sky above and the earth below, for there might be a significance in what I saw that I could not guess unless I observed it very carefully and sincerely. So I would pause each time I came back to the center after praying at one of the four directions and look about me very observingly, quietly seeing all living things, the sky and the earth, as manifestations of the Great Spirit and His marvelous power and knowledge.

Thus I watched the red and black ants crawling over bits of sticks and the rocks on the ground, searching for food or carrying what food they

found back to their nests and I marvelled at their industry and cooperation. On a rock a little short-horned lizard was sunning itself, the eyes
blinking in the dying sunlight, but when a fly buzzed down and lit upon
the rock, the lizard jumped like a flash and seized it. Then, as if surprised
at its own action, or perhaps fearing a bird enemy, it jumped down and
ran to hide under a twisting pine root. Next, a most beautiful fly,
reddish-brown in color and with bright green eyes, landed on my pipestem and regarded me solemnly. I could see even the tiny hairs on its
legs and watched as it carefully cleansed its head with one of the claws at
the tip of a front leg. After it had gone a loud cry drew my eyes above me
to a large bird sweeping up and over the mountain top at incredible
speed, but the glimpse I had of its brown body, long sharp-pointed wings
with white bars near the dark tips, white throat and wide mouth, made
me sure it was a nighthawk.

The importance of observing these creatures closely came home to
me in a flash of insight that this was increasing my sensitivity—lack of
sensitivity was the principal reason for man losing contact with the
Spirit. When I later saw a golden eagle soaring towards us out of the
west, and then dipping low until it disappeared in a sudden swift dive
after some prey hidden below on the mountainside, I watched every
detail of dip and quiver of pinion. I knew the Sioux as well as other
Indian peoples believe the eagle is the greatest visible symbol of man's
potential spiritual power, since the eagle climbs highest of all birds in the
sky and by his climbing warns us how we too must climb up and up from
the things of the earth that hold us down spiritually until we lose these
clinging impediments forever.

Far to the west on the edge of the sky a few clouds were gathering and
into these the sun sank in glory, painting them with gold and scarlet,
which gradually turned paler and then to dark purple as the sun slipped
below the horizon and the wings of night began to spread over the earth.
It was a magic moment, and I sent my prayers out stronger than ever
towards the west.

How can I tell you of that strange night on Bear Butte, with the stars
more clean and bright than I had ever seen them, revolving in slow
majesty above me as the hours passed. I did a lot of standing up and
walking and praying that night, for the rocks under my sagebrush bed
were very sharp and not conducive to rest, while after midnight the wind
blew hard and cold out of the northwest, singing shrilly through the pine
needles. This was the time of great testing, for my temptation was to
stand still and begin to shiver and shake, since the single flimsy blanket
was little protection against that wind. But I remembered what one old
Indian had told me long ago, "Throw your spirit out when the wind

comes cold, and it will bring the blood rushing to the outer parts of your body, keeping them warm, but if you become afraid of the cold and suck your bodily forces inward, your outer parts will freeze!''

So I concentrated on singing my prayers outward as hard as I could as if my spirit were rushing out in all directions, and gradually the initial overwhelming tendency to shiver stopped. I grew tired after about two o'clock and realized I needed some rest before the dawn came. Fools Crow had warned me that "it is most important to greet the daybreak star with songs and prayers just before the dawn comes and then sing in the coming of the dawn, for this symbolizes the coming back of the Spirit to mankind, which the whole world needs.'' So I lay down on my rocky bed and tried to sleep, though it was nearly impossible because of the rocks stabbing into my back no matter what way I turned. But somehow, four times I managed to find a snatch of sleep that night and in each of those four brief moments of slumber I had a vision.

The first one was perhaps the most strange and weird, yet somehow not frightening. I sensed that a huge man was standing beside me in the darkness, a man of immense power. He soon reached down and placed his arms under my body and lifted me as if I were as light as a fluff of down. Then he carried me about a hundred yards down the mountainside till we came to the opening of a cave. Into this cave he carried me about fifty feet, it seemed, until we came to a room that was filled with a suffused light. The room was carpeted deeply with sweet-smelling sagebrush, sacred to the Sioux, and on this he placed me. As I felt myself sinking into that softness, for this sagebrush bed was far deeper and softer than my primitive bed of sagebrush on the mountain top, I felt surrounded by warmth, comfort and protection, a most happy contented feeling after the cold wind and the sharp rocks above. As I lay there he spoke to me six words: "Here you will be all right!''

Soon, however, I woke once more to the cold wind and the sharp rocks of the mountain top, and wondered about the meaning of my strange dream. Fools Crow explained it later.

In my second vision I saw briefly and yet with the utmost clarity and beauty, what appeared to be a king or milk snake coiled in a perfect coil, with nine coils from tail to head. Something induced me to count those coils. The exquisite colors of the snake were in perfect balance, a series of wide red bands each surrounded by two narrower black bands that were also on both sides of medium-sized white and yellow bands. The yellow bands were most noticeable in the middle part of the snake, while the white bands were found mainly at the two extremes near the tail and head. I knew instantly what this beautiful vision meant without having to be told. The nine coils were the nine religions of the world coming together in harmony, while the red, black, white and yellow bands indicated the four major races of the world also coming together in unity. The white bands being mainly nearer the head and tail ends, meant many whites would come into this harmony early, while another very large population of them would come into the circle of harmony much later. The yellow people, the dream seemed to say, would come evenly all the way. Considering the strong prejudice of many white people towards other races, this prediction seems of merit.

My third and fourth visions can only be told here in part, as the time to tell all about them awaits some later day. In the third vision I saw a tall round hat with a strip of buffalo skin around the lower part of the crown. This hat became lost and I realized that because it had great spiritual power, the loss was very dangerous. Many people helped look for it, the search becoming quite desperate, but I eventually found it.

In the fourth vision I was seated at a round table, like the round table of King Arthur, with many Indians seated around it, while I was the only white. The leader at the head of the table smoked a sacred pipe to the seven directions, then passed the pipe so it went completely around the table, being smoked equally by each person there. That is all I can tell about my four visions at present.

After waking from the fourth vision I saw a very brilliant star, the Daybreak Star, shining in the east to signify the dawn was near, and I began again my prayers and songs to the seven directions and around and around the sacred circle. But each time I faced the Daybreak Star I threw my spirit toward it with all my force, as I realized that it symbolized the coming of a very Sacred Being, as is said by Jesus in the Bible, *Revelation* 22:16: "I am the root and the offspring of David, and the bright and morning star."

The coming of the dawn was slow at first, a slight graying on the horizon, then the beginning of yellow light, then the clouds in the east turning light yellow and pink, then glorious golden and scarlet, and the whole rim of the sky circling now with pulsing fire. I was singing as if my heart would burst, and I heard David singing too. So we greeted that glorious sunrise from the top of the Sacred Mountain, and it seemed to me in that moment that earth and sky joined to welcome not just a new day of the sun, but a new and wonderful day for all mankind!

David also had had visions that same night, so we stayed singing and praying on the mountain top until near evening of that second day, then climbed down the steep trail to find Fools Crow waiting for us at the bottom. He told us that he had had two visions while we were up there, though the second could have been the real thing. In his first vision he saw and felt the whole mountain shaking as if with a great earthquake.

He believed this indicated something tremendous was happening that night, but something which we would not really know about until years later. The second vision was very realistic but he was not sure whether he dreamed it or not. It was the sight of a tall Indian striding up the mountain towards the lesser of the two peaks. This Indian was dressed completely in the old way of long ago, and he looked very majestic and noble. Fools Crow felt this meant the Sacred Mountain was accepting our vigils on the mountain top in the way the Spirit did of old.

David Moore said of his three interesting visions:

"In my first vision I saw the strikingly rugged bluffs, hills and canyons of the Badlands of South Dakota, as if I were gazing on them from the sky, and with their glorious colors stretching away beneath me to the edge of the world. Directly below me I saw a steep bluff along the bottom of which ran an old dirt wagon road. I knew instantly that this road signified my own path which led through these Badlands to some destiny not yet seen.

"In my second vision I saw a great cliff of iron that seemed to hang in the air like a huge slab and on its top was the massive and powerfully muscled figure of a Buffalo Man. His body and face were man-like, but he had the mane of a buffalo on his shoulders and back of his head, while the head itself had two great horns. He was facing to my right and had dancing ornaments on both ankles and wrists which were waving and shaking and ringing as he danced with a feeling of immense power. In his left hand he held a carved rod of various colors that I knew was his rod of spirit power and which he was shaking also. Fools Crow told me this vision was very 'washtai', but that he could not tell me the meaning until he himself had vision help about it.

"My third vision was even stranger. I found myself standing in an underground tunnel or hall of which one wall was made of rock blocks about one times two feet each in size, all covered with very moist hangings of moss, as if this were the base of some very ancient cathedral or abby or temple. There was a niche in the center of this wall which held a cake or patty of meat. I seemed to float near to this niche and saw there was a jewel box on top of the cake and that this box was lined with beautiful blue silk. Upright on this silk was a plain golden ring, which, before my eyes, turned into a key ring and next to it appeared a five-pointed silver star that gradually melted and reshaped into a nine-pointed star. I knew without being told that this meant that the nine-pointed star was the key to the future of the world.

"Fools Crow said about all these visions that they were "very wash-tai!' "

When I told Fools Crow about my four visions, he repeated several times after each one the words: "Washtai! Washtai"! (very good, very good), and for the second one he said: "Washtai wakan!" (very holy!). He accepted my explanation of the second vision, but of the first one (about the man carrying me) which had mystified me, he said: "It means the Spirit of the Sacred Mountain, which is really a representative of the Great Spirit, accepted you wholeheartedly for you came with purified heart and mind and tried for your vision in the right way." The two last visions, which I cannot give completely in this book, I hope will be explained someday later. Nevertheless there is every evidence their meaning is most good.

It is interesting that the nine sacred coils or circles of my second vision are foretold in the legend of White Buffalo Calf Maiden (see Chapter Eight), and also in the legend of King Arthur, when Merlin was put to sleep in the secret cave in the Mountains of Wales, and was told by the sacred woman that they represented the coming back of the Logres, the Circle of Harmony that had died with the smashing of King Arthur's Round Table (see also Chapter Nine).

chapter NINETEEN

A Warning from the Thunder Beings

It is lovely indeed, it is lovely indeed.
I, I am the spirit within the earth . . .
The feel of the earth are my feet. . .
The legs of the earth are my legs. . .
The bodily strength of the earth is my strength. . .
The thoughts of the earth are my thoughts. . .
The voice of the earth is my voice. . .
The feather of the earth is my feather. . .
All that belongs to the earth belongs to me. . .
All that surrounds the earth surrounds me. . .
I, I am the sacred words of the earth. . .
It is lovely indeed, it is lovely indeed.

"Song of the Earth Spirit," Origin Legend of the Navajo.
Page 124 in *Navajo Wildlands*, Ballantine Books-Sierra Club, San Francisco, 1969.

SAY THE INDIANS OF LONG ago: "The Thunder Beings are the Voice of the Sky Father; they bring the rain to make the earth grow, but they also send warnings."

I believe the Thunder Beings are warning us today. I think they are saying something like this:

"Look up, look down, feel the sky, feel the earth, feel all living things. Be still as the waters of a pond and listen; be watchful as the eagle over his children; be alert to the inner meanings in the trees, in the stars, in the moon, in the sun, in the rainbow, in the waterfall, in the thunder, in the lightning, in the falling rain, in the other plant people, in the winged peoples, in the four-legged peoples, and the six-legged, and last of all the two-leggeds.

"Do you think you are put on this earth just to do what you please, like the child who wants his mother to give him everything he wants? This is not the freedom you may think it is. Instead it is slavery, terrible slavery to every passion, every whim, every desire. This is what drags down the man, drags down the family, drags down the nation, drags down the civilization, could destroy the world. Men like the powerful dictators are men who could destroy the earth in their thirst for power, more and more power. They are men who never grow up; they are still children, but they could play with other people as a cruel child tortures a poor little kitten.

"You need a new spiritual strength to help change the world, changing it not by force, not by brainwashing, not by fear or hate, but by love, understanding, purity and by the power of example. So go into the wilderness; leave the city; leave the smog; leave the smelly waters and streets. Find a mountain or at least a hill or hidden vale where all about you is quiet. Be still, think, feel the beauty and power of earth and sky. Realize there is too little of this left, too little wildlife left, too few forests and woods left, too few crystal streams singing down the canyons, and much too much ugliness in the hearts and minds and places all over the world. Is it not time for a great change?

"Listen, watch, feel, think, be still, controlled, forget your desires as if they were deadly poison, as many of them are! This civilization has put the whole earth in terrible danger by its over-exploitation of living things, by its burning of fuels that pollute the air, by its poisoning of the waters, its creation of erosion and deserts, by its corruption of governments and men. Are automobiles, airplanes, superhighways, and all the other fancy gadgets that have seemed so important to us, really worth more to you than a liveable, beautiful earth? Maybe by hard work and scientific inventions you can save a lot of your comforts, too, by developing new energy sources and ways of living that don't pollute and destroy. But think things through. Don't just blindly insist you must merrily continue on your way, demanding every luxury and refusing any sacrifice because you want what you want, like the greedy child consuming a box of candy without thought of the stomachache coming. The people of the world may soon wake up with something a lot worse than a bad stomach if they continue with their present reckless consumption, exploitation and destruction.

"Stop, think, grasp yourself as if with a mighty hand; hold yourself in this hand; look at yourself! Look at yourself when you were a little child, when life was simple and pure and good; when you had such promise to be a wonderful human being. You still have the choice to change, to work with will and spirit to get the world started on a new trail, a new road where simple honesty is more important than a million dollars, where a tree saved to give beauty and oxygen to the earth is better even than the boards to build a home unless that use can be done with balance, where a bird flying high in the sky can be understood to give more value to man in spirit power than a thousand guns that might be used to shoot it.

"Choose strong, choose with courage, and join the fight. It is the most glorious battle in all history, the fight to help all cultures flower with distinctive beauty, every child to be given the chance to feel and understand the magic of the wild and to fulfill its destiny as a creative human being, every man and woman to become part of a great and glorious purpose, to make the earth beautiful, united in justice and harmony, unified but diversified, law-abiding without the use of club or gun, and filled with understanding and love.

Bibliography

Religious Books:

1. Ashe, Arthur. *The Quest for Arthur's Britain.* New York City, Praeger. 1968.

2. Esele, Ives. *The Invisible Pyramid.* New York City. Charles Scribners Sons. 1970.

3. Furst, Peter T. Edited by. *Flesh of the Gods.* New York City. Praeger Publications. 1972.

4. Green, Roger R. *King Arthur and His Knights of the Round Table.* Baltimore. Penguin Books. 1953.

5. Hays, H.R. *In the Beginning–Early Man and His Gods.* New York City. C. P. Putnam and Sons. 1963.

6. Jung, Emma. *The Grail Legend.* London. Hodder & Stoughton. 1971.

7. Lowie, Robert H. *Primitive Religion.* New York City. Liveright Publishing Co. 1924, 1948.

8. Saklatvala, Beram. *Arthur, Roman Britain's Last Champion.* New York City. Taplinger. 1967.

9. Von Greenebaum, G. E. and Callois, Roger. Edited by. *The Dream and Human Societies.* Berkeley. U of Calif. Press. 1966.

Special Books on Indians:

10. Armstrong, Virginia Irving. Compiled by. *I Have Spoken–American Indians Through the Voices of the Indians*. Beverly Hills. Sage Books. 1971.

11. Collier, James Lincoln. *Do Plants Have Feelings Too?* (article—Readers Digest, April, 1972.)

12. Hertzberg, Hazel W. *The Search for an American Indian Identity*. Syracuse University Press. 1971.

13. Jones, Louis Thomas. *Aboriginal American Oratory*. Southwest Museum, Los Angeles. 1965.

14. Mead, Margaret. *Changing Culture of an Indian Tribe*. New York City. AMS Press. 1932.

15. Sherris, Earl. *Death of the Great Spirit: An Elegy for the American Indian*. New York City. Simon and Schuster, Inc. 1971.

16. Spicer, Edward H. Edited by. *Perspectives in American Indian Cultural Change*. U of Chicago Press. 1961.

General Works:

17. Driver, Harold E. *Indians of North America* (2nd Ed.). U of Chicago Press. 1969.

18. Forbes, Jack D. Edited by. *The Indian in America's Past*. Englewood Cliffs, N.J. Prentice-Hall, Inc. 1964.

19. Garland, Hamlin. *Book of the American Indian*. New York City. Garrett Press. 1971.

20. Owen, Roger C., Deetz, James J.F., Fisher, Anthony D. *The North American Indians: A Source Book*. New York City. Macmillan, Inc. 1968.

21. Radin, Paul. *Indians of South America*. Westport, Conn. Greenwood Press, Inc. 1942.

22. Stewart, Julian H. Edited by. *Handbook of South American Indians*. New York City. Cooper Square. 1957.

23. Steward, Julian H. and Faron, Louis C. *Native Peoples of South America*. New York City. McGraw-Hill. 1959.

24. Swanton, John R. *The Indian Tribes of North America*. Smithsonian Institution Press. 1969.

25. Underhill, Ruth M. *Red Man's America*. U of Chicago Press. 1971.

26. Vazquez, Pedro Ramirez. *Mexico*. New York City. Harry N. Abrams, Inc. 1968.

Special Books—Indian Religion and Mythology:

27. Alexander, Hartley B. *North American Mythology*. New York City. Cooper Square. 1964.

28. Alexander, Hartley B. *Latin American Mythology*. New York City. Cooper Square. 1964.

29. Alexander, Hartley B. *The World's Rim: Great Mysteries of the North American Indians*. Lincoln. U of Nebraska Press. 1967.

30. Barrett, S.A. *Pomo Myths*. Milwaukee. Bulletin, Public Museum. 1933.

31. Benedict, Ruth Fulton. *The Concept of the Guardian Spirit in North America*. Washington, D. C. Memoirs of the American Anthropological Ass'n. 1928.

32. Braden, Charles S. *Religious Aspects of the Conquest of Mexico*. New York City. AMS Press. 1930.

33. Brown, Joseph Epes. Edited by. *The Sacred Pipe: Black Elk's Account of the Seven Rites of the Oglala Sioux*. Norman. U of Oklahoma Press. 1967.

34. Brown, Joseph E. *Spiritual Legacy of the American Indian*. Wallingford, Pa. Pendle Hill. 1964.

35. Brown, Vinson. *Great Upon the Mountain: Crazy Horse of America*. Healdsburg, Calif. Naturegraph Publishers. 1971.

36. Castaneda, Carlos. *Journey to Ixtlan: Lessons of Don Juan*. New York City. Simon and Schuster, Inc. 1972.

37. Castaneda, Carlos. *Teachings of Don Juan: A Yaqui Way of Knowledge*. Berkeley. U of Calif. Press, 1968.

38. Clark, Cora. Collected by. *Pomo Indian Myths*. New York City. Vantage Press, Inc. 1954.

39. Clark, Ella E. *Indian Legends of the Pacific Northwest*. Berkeley. U of Calif. Press. 1969.

40. Clark, Ella E. *Indian Legends From the Northern Rockies*. Norman. U of Oklahoma Press. 1967.

41. Eastman, Charles Alexander. *The Soul of the Indian*. Rapid City, S.D. Fenwyn Press Books.

42. Giddings, Ruth Warner. *Yaqui Myths and Legends*. Tucson. U of Arizona Press. 1959.

43. Goetz, Delia and Morley, Sylvanus. *Popol Vuh: The Sacred Book of the Ancient Quiche Maya*. Norman. U of Oklahoma Press. 1969.

44. Guiteras-Holmes, Calixta. *Perils of the Soul*. New York City. Free Press. 1961.

45. Hedrick, Basil Calvin. *Quetzalcoatl*. (Occasional papers in Nasoamerican Anthropology, No. 1.) Carbondale, Illinois. Museum of Southern Illinois University. 1967.

46. Henry, Thomas R. *Wilderness Messiah, the Story of Hiawatha of the Iroquois*. Wm. Sloan Assoc. 1955.

47. Hurdy, John Major. *American Indian Religions*. Los Angeles. Shenburne Press, Inc. 1970.

48. Keeler, Clyde E. *Apples of Immortality From the Cuna Tree of Life*. Jericho, N.Y. Exposition. 1961.

49. Kilpatrick, Jack F. and Kilpatrick, Anna G. *Run Toward the Nightland: Magic of the Oklahoma Cherokees*. Dallas, Southern Methodist University Press. 1967.

50. Kluckhohn, Clyde. *Navaho Witchcraft*. Boston, Beacon Press. 1962.

51. Kroeber, A.L. *The Religions of the Indians of California*. Berkeley. U of Calif. publication in Archaeology and Ethnology. Vol. 4, No. 6. 1906.

52. La Barre, Weston. *Peyote Cult*. New York City. Schocken Books, Inc. 1969.

53. Landes, Ruth. *Ojibwa Religion and the Midewiwin*. Madison. U of Wisconsin Press. 1968.

54. Link, Margaret Schevill. Retold by. *The Pollen Path: A Collection of Navajo Myths*. Stanford U Press. 1956.

55. Lone Dog, Louise. *Strange Journey*. Healdsburg, Calif. Naturegraph Publishers. 1964.

56. Makemson, Maud. *The Book of the Jaguar Priest*. New York City. Abelard Schuman Pub. 1951.

57. Marriott, Alice and Rachlin, Carol K. *Peyote*. New York City. T.Y. Crowell. 1971.

58. Masson, Marcelle. *A Bag of Bones: Legends of the Wintu Indians*. Healdsburg, Calif. Naturegraph Publishers. 1966.

59. McLuhan, T.C. *Touch the Earth*. New York City. Outerbridge. 1971.

60. Metiraux, Alfred. *Myths of the Toba and Pilaga*. Austin, Tex. American Folklore Society. 1946.

61. Mooney, James. *Ghost Dance Religion and the Sioux Outbreak of 1890*. U of Chicago Press. 1965.

62. Moriarty, James R. *Chinigchinix: An Indigenous California Indian Religion*. Los Angeles. Southwest Museum. 1969.

63. Nicholson, Irene. *Mexican and Central American Mythology*. New York City. Tudor Publishing Group. 1967.

64. Osborne, Harold. *South American Mythology*. New York City. Tudor Publishing Group. 1968.

65. Powell, Peter. Edited by. *Sweet Medicine: The Continuing Role of The Sacred Arrows, The Sun Dance, and the Sacred Buffalo Hat in Northern Cheyenne History*. Norman. U of Oklahoma Press. 1969.

66. Reichard, Gladys A. *Navajo Religion: Study of Symbolism*. Princeton University Press. 1964.

67. Roys, Ralph L. *The Book of Chilam Balam of Chumayel*. Norman. U of Oklahoma Press. 1967.

68. Seton, Ernest Thompson and Julia M. *The Gospel of the Redman: A Way of Life*. Santa Fe, N.M. Seton Village. 1966.

69. Shearer, Tony. *Lord of the Dawn: Quetzalcoatl*. Healdsburg, Calif. Naturegraph Publishers. 1971.

70. Squire, Roger. *Wizards and Wampum: Legends of the Iroquois*. New York City. Abelard-Schuman Ltd. 1971.

71. Tyler, Hamilton A. *Pueblo Gods and Myths*. Norman. U of Oklahoma Press. 1964.

72. Underhill, Ruth M. *Red Man's Religion*. U of Chicago Press. 1965.

73. Villsenor, David. *Tapestries in Sand: The Spirit of the Indian Sandpainting*. Healdsburg, Calif. Naturegraph Publishers. 1966.

74. Wallace, Paul A. *White Roots of Peace*. Port Washington, N.Y. Ira J. Friedman. 1968.

75. Whiting, Beatrice B. *Paiute Sorcery*. New York City. Johnson Reprint Corp. 1963.

76. Willoya, Williams and Brown, Vinson. *Warriors of the Rainbow*. Healdsburg, Calif. Naturegraph Publishers. 1962.

Special Books on Tribes:

77. Alphonse, Ephraim S. *A Guaymi Grammar and Dictionary With Some Ethnological Notes*. Smithsonian Institution, Bureau of American Ethnology Bulletin 162.

78. Bass, Althea. *The Arapaho Way: A Memoir of an Indian Boyhood*. New York City. Clarkson N. Potter, Inc. 1966.

79. Caso, Alfonso. *Aztecs, People of the Sun*. Norman. U of Oklahoma Press. 1970.

80. Faron, Luis C. *Hawks of the Sun (Aztecs)*. U of Pittsburgh Press. 1970.

81. Culbert T. Patrick. Edited by. *The Classic Maya Collapse*. Albuquerque. U of New Mexico Press. 1973.

82. Grinnell, George Bird. *The Cheyenne Indians: Their History and Way of Life*. New Haven. Yale University Press. 1923.

83. Keeler, Clyde E. *Land of the Moon Children: The Primitive San Blas Culture in Flux*. Athens. U of Georgia Press. 1956.

84. Kroeber, Theodore. *Ishi in Two Worlds*. Berkeley. U of California Press. 1967.

85. Linderman, Frank B. *Plenty Coups, Chief of the Crows*. Lincoln. U of Nebraska Press. 1962.

86. Lurie, Nancy O. Edited by. *Mountain Wolf Woman, Sister of Crashing Thunder: Autobiography of a Winnebago Indian*. Ann Arbor. U of Michigan Press. 1961.

87. Marriott, Alice. *Saynday's People*. Lincoln. U of Nebraska Press. 1963.

88. Marriott, Alice. *The Ten Grandmothers*. Norman. U of Oklahoma Press. 1968.

89. Neihardt, John G. (Flaming Rainbow). *Black Elk Speaks*. Lincoln. U of Nebraska Press. 1961.

90. Opler, Morris Edward. *An Apache Life-Way*. New York City. Cooper Square. 1965.

91. Portilla, Miguel Leon. *Aztec Thought and Culture*. Norman. U of Oklahoma Press. 1956; 1963.

92. Hyde, Philip and Jett, Stephen C. *Navajo Wildlands*. New York City. Sierra Club, Ballantine Book.

93. Radin Paul. *Autobiography of a Winnebago Indian*. New York City. Dover. 1920.

94. Sandoz, Mari. *Crazy Horse*. Lincoln. U of Nebraska Press. 1961.

95. Shipek, Florence C. *Autobiography of Delfina Cuero: Diegueno Indian*. Los Angeles. Dawson's Book Shop. 1968.

96. Spicer, Edward H. *Yaqui*. U of Chicago Press. 1961.

97. Stands-in-Timber, John and Liberty, Margot. *Cheyenne Memories*. New Haven, Conn. Yale University Press. 1967.

98. Thompson, J. Eric. *Maya Hieroglyphic Writing*. Norman. U of Oklahoma Press. 1960.

99. Underhill, Ruth M. *The Navajos*. Norman. U of Oklahoma Press. 1967.

110. Vasquez, Pedro Ramirez and others. *Toltec Art and Archaeology*. New York City. Henry N. Abrams, Inc. 1968.

101. Wallace, Anthony F. C. *The Death and Rebirth of the Seneca*. New York City. Knopf. 1969.

102. Waters, Frank. *Pumpkin Seed Point*. Beverly Hills, Calif. Sage Books. 1969.

103. Waters, Frank. *Book of the Hopi*. New York City. Viking Press. 1964.

104. Waltfish, Gene. *The Lost Universe*. New York City. Basic Books. 1965.

105. Wilson, Edmund. *Apologies to the Iroquois*. New York City. Farrar, Straus and Giroux. 1960.

106. Wolf, Eric. *Sons of the Shaking Earth*. U of Chicago Press. 1959.

Regional Books on Indians:

107. Forbes, Jack D. *Native Americans of California and Nevada: A Handbook*. Healdsburg, Calif. Naturegraph Publishers. 1969.

108. Forbes, Jack D. *Nevada Indians Speak*. Reno, Nevada. U of Nevada Press. 1967.

109. Hyde, George E. *Indians of the High Plains: From the Prehistoric Period to the Coming of Europeans*. Norman. U of Oklahoma Press. 1970.

110. Hyde, George E. *Indians of the Woodlands, from Prehistoric Times to 1725*. Norman. U of Oklahoma Press. 1970.

111. Kroeber, A. L. *Handbook of the Indians of California*. St. Claire Shores, Mich. Scholarly. 1925.

112. Kroeber, Theodora and Heizer, Robert F. *Almost Ancestors: First Californians*. New York City. Ballantine. 1970.

113. Mails, Thomas E. *The Mystic Warriors of the Plains*. Garden City, N.Y. Doubleday. 1972.

114. Means, Philip A. *Ancient Civilizations of the Andes*. Staten Island, N.Y. Gordian. 1964.

115. Paddock, John. Edited by. *Ancient Oaxaca, Discoveries in Mexican Archaeology and History*. Stanford University Press. 1966.

116. Soustelle, Jacques, *The Four Suns*. New York City. Grossman. 1971.

117. Swanton, John R. *Indian Tribes of Mexico, Central America and the West Indies*. Seattle, Wash. Shorey. 1952.

118. Wiley, G. R. Edited by. *Handbook of Middle American Indians*. Austin, Texas. U of Texas Press. 1964.